SHE'S A MENSCH!

TEN AMAZING JEWISH WOMEN

ANNE DUBLIN

SHE'S A

Mensch!

TEN AMAZING JEWISH WOMEN

DO YOU KNOW
?
MY NAME?

Second Story Press

Library and Archives Canada Cataloguing in Publication

Title: She's a mensch! : ten amazing Jewish women / Anne Dublin.
Other titles: She is a mensch!
Names: Dublin, Anne, author.
Description: Series statement: Do you know my name? ; 3 | Includes bibliographical
    references.
Identifiers: Canadiana (print) 20220465355 | Canadiana (ebook) 2022046538X | ISBN
    9781772603200 (softcover) | ISBN 9781772603217 (EPUB)
Subjects: LCSH: Jewish women—Biography—Juvenile literature. | LCGFT: Biographies.
Classification: LCC DS115.2 .D83 2023 | DDC j920.72/089924—dc23

*Second Story Press gratefully acknowledges the support of the Ontario Arts Council
and the Canada Council for the Arts for our publishing program. We acknowledge
the financial support of the Government of Canada through the Canada Book Fund.*

Conseil des Arts du Canada   Canada Council for the Arts

ONTARIO ARTS COUNCIL
CONSEIL DES ARTS DE L'ONTARIO
an Ontario government agency
un organisme du gouvernement de l'Ontario

Funded by the Government of Canada
Financé par le gouvernement du Canada

Canada

Published by
Second Story Press
20 Maud Street, Suite 401
Toronto, ON
M5V 2M5
www.secondstorypress.ca

MIX
Paper from
responsible sources
FSC® C103567

To people everywhere who strive to make our world a better place.

Hope is like a path in the countryside: originally there was no path—
yet, as people are walking all the time in the same spot, a way appears.

—Attributed to Chinese essayist, Lu Xun, 1921[1]

It is not up to you to finish the work, yet you are not free to avoid it.

—Rabbi Tarfon, *Pirkei Avot (Ethics of our Fathers)*
Chapter 2:16[2]

CONTENTS

Introduction

You've probably heard of Anne Frank, who wrote her famous *Diary of a Young Girl* while she hid with her family for about two years during the Nazi occupation of the Netherlands. But have you heard of Ágnes Keleti, the Olympic gymnast? Or Pauline Bebe, the first female rabbi in France? Or scientist and human rights activist, Rita Arditti? If these names are new to you, then this is the book for you.

Within the pages of this book, you will read about the lives of ten unsung Jewish women—women who have dedicated their lives to doing remarkable things. The women come from many different countries in the world and work in many different fields. They were all born in the twentieth century. These women are examples of people we can look up to. They made the world a better place.

The chapters are organized from the oldest to the youngest woman, but you can read them in whatever order you like. I enjoyed researching the lives of these amazing women and interviewing some of them and their loved ones. Don't worry if you don't understand all the words and historical terms; they're included in the glossary at the back of this book.

Why did I write *She's a Mensch*? I believe that, by learning about the lives of great Jewish women, we can understand the importance of fighting for human rights and dignity for all. I hope their lives will inspire you to make your own positive impact in the world.

ÁGNES KELETI

1921–

MELBOURNE, AUSTRALIA, 1956

Ágnes took a deep breath. She stared at the uneven parallel bars. They had seemed so high when she was a little girl long ago in Budapest. Now, after so many years when staying alive had been all that mattered, she was, despite her age, trying for Olympic gold. She rubbed the white chalk on the palms of her calloused hands. She took another deep breath, just as her coach always told her she should. She was ready.

Ágnes Edit Keleti was born in Budapest, Hungary on January 9, 1921, to Rózsika and Ferenc Klein. Ferenc was a businessman, a wholesaler of tinned meat. He was also passionate about all kinds of sports—rowing, hiking, fishing, skiing, and mountain climbing—as well as the opera, theater, and classical music.

As Ágnes grew older, she emulated her father in the sports that he loved. When she was four years old, she began training in gymnastics at Budapest's Jewish club. She also enjoyed her school studies, including private lessons in German and English, as well as cello lessons. These activities helped her develop the tenacity, courage, and strength that she would need in the years ahead.

Life wasn't easy under Miklós Horthy, the head of the government in Hungary. In 1933, Adolf Hitler and his Nazi party came to power in Germany. Beginning in 1938, Hungary's leaders began to enact anti-Jewish laws similar to those in Germany. It became harder for Ágnes to go to school as well as to continue her gymnastics training. Soon afterwards, her father, Ferenc, lost control of his business. He was devastated; a broken man. The Klein family were forced to move to an apartment in a poorer neighborhood of the city.

In 1939, when she was eighteen years old, Ágnes completed high school. Although she had good grades, she wasn't allowed to go to university or technical college. She was very disappointed because the antisemitic quota system drastically limited the number of Jews who were admitted. So, Ágnes had to find a job to help support herself. She became an apprentice to a furrier and learned the skills necessary for making fur garments. At first glance, this trade seemed to be unlucky—a poor alternative to a university education—but it turned out to be one of the best decisions of her life.

Around this time, Ágnes realized that having a Jewish-sounding name left her vulnerable to antisemitic remarks or abuse. So, she changed her name from

Klein to Keleti. But this new name didn't keep her Jewish identity a secret.

During her apprenticeship, Ágnes managed to continue her gymnastics training, but in 1941 she was forced off her gymnastics team because she was Jewish. This was just the beginning of the horror and suffering that was to come.

Germany invaded Hungary in March 1944. Up to this point, Miklós Horthy had refused to deport Hungary's Jews to German concentration camps. He had instead compromised with the German forces by restricting where Jewish people could go and what they could do. But with the German invasion, the relative security of Hungary's Jews came to an end.

The Nazis brought their hatred against the Jews with them and Hungarian Jews soon became victims of the Holocaust. Between May and early July of 1944, approximately 400,000 Hungarian Jews were rounded up and sent to extermination camps in Nazi-occupied Poland. After Ágnes's father and most of her family were sent away to Auschwitz, the concentration/extermination camp in Poland, Ágnes knew that something drastic had to be done.

In those days, everyone was frantically trying to find a safe place to escape or to hide. Ágnes once said that, as soon as she heard of the German occupation, "the thought of escape filled my life."[3] Ágnes's mother, sister Vera, and young nephew Jánoska were lucky to obtain a *Schutzpass*, a safety pass from the Swiss diplomat Carl Lutz. They went into hiding in a safe house until the end of the war.

Ágnes had heard a rumor that young married women would not be deported. So, in April 1944, she married another outstanding Jewish gymnast, István Sárkány. However, their marriage didn't save her husband. Soon afterwards, István was sent to the concentration camp of Mauthausen in Austria. He barely survived the ill treatment and starvation in that notorious camp.

Ágnes had to find another way to save herself. She paid all the money she had to buy the identity of a Christian girl, Piroska Juhász, and lived under this false identity until the war ended in 1945. During that time, she worked as a furrier in Budapest and later in a town called Szalkszentmárton, almost forty miles from Budapest. Every moment of every day, she feared that her true identity would be discovered and that she would be sent away to her death.

She eventually moved to Pesterzsébet, a suburb of Budapest, where she thought she would be safer. There, she found work in an ammunitions factory. Every morning during the Battle of Budapest (December 26, 1944 to February 13, 1945), when the Soviet and Romanian armies were battling German and Hungarian forces, Ágnes helped to collect the bodies of people who had died the previous day and carted them to a mass grave.

When the war in Europe ended on May 8, 1945, Ágnes was alive and able to reunite with her mother and sister and eventually, her husband. (Ágnes and István had an amicable divorce in 1950.) But life was very hard in those early days after the war ended. As Ágnes said, "Our house was hit by a bomb. We lost everything; the factory, half of which was my father's, was taken away from us. Except for my mother and sister, most of our family had perished. We lost everything, really everything. Peace found me with a single set of clothes and a pair of sandals."[4]

But Ágnes was tough and persistent. Nothing would stop her from returning to her passion for gymnastics—even in cold, ill-equipped gymnasiums—and fulfilling her goals. Between 1947 and 1955, she dominated women's gymnastics in Hungary and qualified for the Hungarian Olympic team. Unfortunately, due to a last-minute injury to her ankle, she couldn't compete in the London Olympics in 1948. It was a huge disappointment, but Ágnes didn't give up. At the World University Games of 1949, she won four gold medals, a silver medal, and a bronze. At the 1952 Helsinki Olympic Games, she won four medals—a gold (floor exercises), a silver (combined team event), and two bronze (uneven parallel bars and hand apparatus-team). Ágnes was then thirty-one years old—the age when most gymnasts would have retired a long time ago!

In the 1954 World Championships in Rome, she finished first on the uneven parallel bars and the hand apparatus-team, second in the combined team, and third on the balance beam. Even with all of this success, she still had not reached the highest point of her career. In 1956, when she competed in the Melbourne Olympics, Ágnes was thirty-five years old. Yet she scored an astonishing triumph: She won four gold medals (uneven parallel bars, balance beam, floor exercise, and combined exercise-team) and two silver medals (individual and team all-around competitions). It was an amazing achievement, especially when you consider that there were only seven gymnastic events for women overall in those Olympics *and* she had won more medals than any other woman gymnast at those games! During "normal" times, Ágnes would have returned to her native Hungary as a hero and would have begun a career of teaching and coaching the next generation of gymnasts. But that was not to be.

The Hungarian Revolution had begun on October 23, 1956, with protests by student groups against the oppressive policies of the Soviet Union, which had "liberated" the country from German occupation during World War II but then had taken it over in 1945. Ágnes and the rest of the Olympic team left for Australia on November 6 or 7, in two separate groups, while the anti-Soviet revolution was raging in Hungary. By November 10, the revolution had been savagely crushed.

Along with forty-eight of her teammates, Ágnes decided to defect and seek asylum in Australia. (An added bonus was that her sister, Vera, had moved to Australia almost ten years earlier.) The discipline and training of an elite athlete and her experiences during the war stood her in good stead. She worked in a factory for six months in Sydney, all the while practicing gymnastics and wondering what the future would bring. Then her luck turned again.

A representative from the relatively new State of Israel invited her to demonstrate gymnastics at the fifth Maccabiah Games that were to take place in Tel Aviv in 1957. Afterwards, Ágnes decided to settle in Israel, where she loved swimming in the ocean and running along the beach. Here Ágnes met her second husband, a sports journalist and athlete called Róbert Bíró. They married in 1959 and had two sons—Daniel and Rafael.

From 1958, Ágnes worked as a coach for the Israeli national gymnastics team, an international gymnastics judge, and a physical education teacher at the Wingate Institute for Physical Education and Sport. Both Ágnes and Róbert taught gymnastics at private gyms and at Wingate until Ágnes retired in the 1990s at the age of seventy-five. Sadly, Róbert died of a sudden heart attack in 2006.

Ágnes never let life's challenges stop her. She said, "I have always been an optimistic person, a dreamer in my whole life. These characteristics helped me find my fortune in unfortunate times."[5]

During the more than fifty years that Ágnes lived in Israel, she went through many of the country's toughest moments: the Six-Day War (1967), the murder of eleven Israeli Olympic team members in Munich (1972), and the Yom Kippur War (1973). In spite of those terrible events, Ágnes loved life in Israel. She said that's where she truly felt free.

Ágnes has received many honors during her lifetime. In 1981, she was inducted into the newly founded International Jewish Sports Hall of Fame in Netanya, Israel, and in 2002, she was also inducted into the International Gymnastics Hall of Fame in Oklahoma City. She received numerous other awards, including being named one of Hungary's twelve "Athletes of the Nation" in 2004. In 2017, Ágnes was awarded the Israel Prize, Israel's highest cultural honor, in recognition of being one of the country's leaders of gymnastics for more than fifty years. It's not an exaggeration to say that Ágnes Keleti is the most successful Jewish female athlete in Olympic history.

As of the writing of this book, Ágnes is the oldest living Olympian. On her one hundredth birthday, which she celebrated on January 9, 2021, she said, "I live well, and it's great that I'm still healthy.… And I love life."[6]

RUTH FIRST

1925–1982

JOHANNESBURG, SOUTH AFRICA, 1963

The heavy steel door of her prison cell clanged shut. The sound hammered through Ruth's neck and shoulders, as if echoing out of the cell, along the hall-way, up the stairs, and around the rest of the police station. Her tiny cell and the narrow bed inside it became Ruth's world for the next 117 days.

In the early years of the twentieth century, many Jews left their homes in the Russian "Pale of Settlement"—the area in the western region of the Russian Empire where they had been restricted to live—in order to escape *pogroms* (antisemitic violence) and terrible poverty. Ruth First's family was part of that mass exodus. Her mother, Tilly (Matilda), traveled with her parents to South Africa from Lithuania in 1901. Her father, Julius First, arrived in South Africa from Latvia with his mother and brother in 1907. From his youth, Julius was active in the Communist Party of South Africa. He felt that a better kind of "sharing" society was needed in order to improve people's lives.

Ruth was born in Johannesburg on May 4, 1925. When she was young, she realized that she was living in a "bubble" of wealth and privilege, one that was reserved only for white people. While Ruth was at Jeppe Girls High School in Johannesburg, she joined the Junior Left Book Club in order to read more about communist, or "leftist," philosophy. This move wasn't surprising since both Ruth's parents were fervent communists. Even then, Ruth was determined to do her best to make her country and the world a better place.

In 1942, she enrolled at the University of the Witwatersrand in Johannesburg, where she studied social science. At that time, she met other activists, co-founded the Federation of Progressive Students, and also joined the Young Communist League. One of the people she met there was Nelson Mandela, whose revolutionary work led him to become South Africa's first Black president in 1994. In his autobiography, Mandela recalled that "Many white students went out of their way to make me feel welcome." These students included Ruth, whom he remembered as having "an outgoing personality" and being "a gifted writer."[7]

In 1946, Ruth met Joe Slovo and they were married in 1949. Joe's background was similar to Ruth's. Joe was born in 1926 and had come from Lithuania in 1936 with his mother and sister. Sadly, his mother died in 1938 and soon afterwards, Joe's father abandoned the children. Joe had to quit school and get a job to support himself and his sister. In 1944, while World War II was still raging, Joe lied about his age—he wasn't eighteen yet—and joined the army. He fought in Italy against the Nazis and, when he came home at the age of twenty, he was able to go to university. He became a lawyer a few years later.

Ruth and Joe eventually entered a period of time that their daughter Gillian called "my parents' Camelot years."[8] Gillian was referring to legendary King Arthur and Queen Guinevere's kingdom—a time when everything seemed to be going well for them. The couple had an active social and professional life. Joe practiced law while Ruth worked as a journalist for various newspapers. They had three daughters in quick succession: Shawn, born in 1950, Gillian in 1952, and Robyn in 1953. They led a comfortable, middle-class life as many white South Africans did.

Meanwhile, life was becoming more and more oppressive for Black South Africans, who made up the majority of the population, as well as for minority groups like "colored" people and "Indians." After the election of 1948, the Afrikaner National Party decided to make laws to separate people even more. This policy was called *apartheid*, which in Afrikaans means "apartness."

Ruth and Joe were shocked at the direction their country was heading. New laws were passed whereby the government tried to control the people. People of color were allowed into white territory only to work. They did not have any say in the way the government ran the country where they lived. Futhermore, in 1949, people of different races were forbidden to marry and after 1950, Black Africans had to carry a passbook all the time to show that they had permission to enter "white areas." In 1953, parks, trains, beaches, and public buildings were segregated with signs for "whites" or "non-whites."

According to their daughter Gillian, during the 1950s, Ruth and Joe "broke all the rules."[9] They visited "Black areas" where they weren't allowed to go so that they could see what was really going on. They were shocked at the poverty and hopelessness they witnessed there, for thousands of people had been uprooted from their farms and forced to move into the Black "Homelands" where they had few opportunities to earn a living or get an education.

At that time, Ruth was writing for newspapers that spoke against apartheid. When the newspaper was banned by the government, the paper would change its name and she would keep on writing. When the Communist Party of South Africa was banned in 1950, Ruth and Joe and other members secretly started it up again.

Even though Ruth and Joe were resisting the new harsh laws, they were still white and well-off. They lived in a three-bedroom bungalow in a middle-class suburb of Johannesburg. As Gillian recalled, it had a big garden overlooking an open *veld*, or field, and a huge, spreading broad-leafed plane tree that the girls used to climb.[10] That's not all. Black domestic workers did the cleaning, cooking, and took care of the little girls. Gillian described it like this: "We lived in a world beset by contradictions.... We were privileged white South African children, serviced by servants, attending whites-only schools...and our parents were plotting to overthrow the state."[11] (These kinds of contradictions were not uncommon, for many white people employed Black Africans in their homes as domestic workers, nannies, gardeners, and so on.)

In those days, many anti-apartheid activists were Jewish but not necessarily practicing Jews. Ruth had been raised by parents who were fervent communists; so, it's not surprising that she shared their attitude about religion. According to communist ideology, the State is where people should have their primary allegiance; organized religion needs to be suppressed, if not eliminated. In an interview years later, Gillian stated, "My parents were communists, so we were brought up in absolutely none of the religious aspects of Judaism…. We were taught to look at the world in terms of social justice."[12]

In 1955, along with members of the African National Congress and its allies, Ruth helped to formulate the Freedom Charter, which spelled out their vision of South Africa as a multiracial society. However, in the following year, the government arrested 156 leaders from the various groups who had supported the Charter. Ruth was among those arrested, but she was released on bail. A long legal battle followed these arrests. The Treason Trial, as it became known, lasted for five years and ended in acquittals for all the accused in 1961.

Ruth's life became more and more restricted. In 1961, she received a "banning order": She had to stay in Johannesburg, couldn't write anything that would be published, and couldn't communicate with other banned people. (Her husband Joe left the country in 1963 and wouldn't return until 1990 when he was granted amnesty.) Ruth's daughters were still young and she needed to support the family. She enrolled in a librarian program at her former university, the University of the Witwatersrand. She hoped she and her family would be safe.

In August 1963, Ruth was arrested and thrown into jail for ninety days. The government had recently passed the "Ninety Day Law," which allowed the security police to arrest anyone they thought was working against the government and detain them for that period. During her imprisonment, she was kept in solitary confinement in an eight-foot cell. No charges were laid; she had no lawyer to help her. She couldn't have visitors or any access to the outside world. She wasn't allowed to talk with the other prisoners or the guards. As she lay on the lumpy mattress, she felt that she was "closed inside a matchbox."[13] She worried that she might be charged with treason; that she would be imprisoned for the rest of her life or even put to death.

During that time, Ruth's mother, Tilly, took care of Ruth's daughters. (Her father Julius was afraid he would be arrested, too, so he had escaped soon after Ruth was jailed.) She even delivered food and clothes to Ruth every day.

Ruth was finally released after ninety days but was rearrested immediately afterwards. On the day of her second arrest, she sat on the edge of the bed. She was still wearing her new navy blue suit that Tilly had bought for the occasion of her release. Ruth shook with sobs, for she had no idea when or if she would be released. She stayed in that prison for another twenty-seven days. During her imprisonment, Ruth felt increasingly desperate. At one point, she even tried to take her own life. That incident was followed by days of hysterical crying. Finally, she began to be resigned to a life in solitary confinement.

When she was finally released in December 1963, "Tilly and the girls were horrified at her condition."[14] Ruth had deteriorated, emotionally and physically, while she was in prison. She felt lost. After her release, she wasn't allowed to meet anyone who mattered to her. (Most of her friends had been banned or jailed or had left the country.) She knew she had to get out of the country. It took months to get permission to leave and even then, she could not get a passport. Finally, the house was sold and their bags were packed. In the middle of the night on March 14, 1964, Ruth and her daughters drove across the border to Swaziland. Ruth would never return to her native country.

◊

The story was not over. Although the girls went to school in Swaziland, Ruth still felt that she was being watched by the South African security police. She even wore a red wig and dark glasses in order to disguise herself! However, she soon realized she would have to leave Africa altogether.

After five or six months in Swaziland, Ruth and the girls made their way to London, England. There, they were finally reunited with Joe. They lived in a house and, on the surface, were an "ordinary" family. But Ruth and Joe were anything but ordinary.

Although the African National Congress (ANC) paid for Joe's food, clothes, and travel costs, Ruth was the breadwinner for the family. She worked hard as a freelance journalist and author, writing numerous articles, pamphlets, reports, and speeches. One of her first books, *117 Days*, told about the time she had been imprisoned. Ruth traveled to other parts of Africa and wrote about important issues. For example, in her book, *The Barrel of a Gun*, she wrote about military coups and the failure of independence struggles in Africa. Ruth was also busy working as a researcher and an editor. She edited Nelson Mandela's autobiography, *No Easy Walk to Freedom*, as well as that of Oginga Odinga, a Kenyan freedom fighter and politician, titled *Not Yet Uhuru*.

Starting in 1972, Ruth took various teaching jobs at universities. For one year, she taught sociology at the University of Manchester, and the following year began teaching women's studies at Durham University in northern England. By that time, her daughters had grown up and left home and Joe was often away for long stretches of time, for he was still secretly working on behalf of the ANC.

In 1977, an opportunity came along that Ruth decided to take. She became professor and research director at the Centre for African Studies at Eduardo Mondlane University in Maputo, the capital of newly independent Mozambique.

In order to work there, Ruth had to learn Portuguese as well as a new way of life. Previously, she had enjoyed expensive clothes, Italian shoes, and weekly visits to the hairdresser. In Mozambique, her needs became much simpler. Now she occupied herself with practical items like getting a good hairbrush or cleaning products.[15]

She loved her new job. As Gillian wrote: "Now finally she had found a home that would accept her talents, her brilliant mind, her fierce commitment, her long experience. She felt validated; she could be herself."[16] However, the South African secret police were still watching Ruth. They feared she might incite people's unrest and anger against the cruel system of apartheid and thus the South African (white) government would lose its power.

On August 17, 1982, Ruth was in her office at the university. She was chatting with a few colleagues when she opened an envelope addressed to her. The envelope contained a letter bomb. "Windows shattered, a hole was torn in the wall, the steel desk was snapped in half and the concrete ceiling cracked.... Ruth, who was bending over the desk, took the full force of the blast and was dead."[17]

In his autobiography, *Long Walk to Freedom*, Nelson Mandela wrote about the courage of the ordinary men and women of his country and of the heroes who helped bring about the great transformation to freedom.

Ruth First was one of those heroes.

MARION WIESEL

1931–

MIAMI, UNITED STATES, 1960s

Marion was sitting on the bus when an elderly Black woman carrying a lot of packages got on the bus. Marion stood up and gave her seat to the woman. The driver shouted that she couldn't do that. Marion felt angry and afraid. She decided to do something about the racism that existed in her adopted country.

Marion Erster Rose Wiesel was born in Vienna, Austria on January 27, 1931. Her parents were Emil and Jetty Erster. Her father owned a furniture store with her uncle. They lived the life of comfortable "middle-class" Jews. One of Marion's favorite pastimes was going to a park close to home where she would gather chestnuts that had fallen from the beautiful trees.[18]

However, when Marion was seven years old, everything changed. The Nazis thought that Austria should be part of "Greater Germany," so they decided to take over Austria on March 12, 1938, in what was called the *Anschluss*.

Marion remembers standing with her father on a bridge over the Danube River as they watched German soldiers march into Vienna. Emil said, "Wait. You'll see something."[19] Around 200,000 cheering Austrians were waving Nazi flags as they greeted the bedraggled German troops entering Marion's beloved city on March 15.

The antisemitic campaign against the Jews began immediately after the *Anschluss*. The Nuremberg Laws were applied in Austria from May 1938, and were later reinforced with innumerable decrees: Jews were gradually robbed of their freedoms and blocked from almost all professions, such as law and teaching. Jewish children like Marion were forced to leave their schools and go to all-Jewish schools. Marion remembers that she had to wear the yellow star on her jacket to identify her as a Jew. For the first time in her life, Marion felt she wasn't as "good as anyone else."[20]

Shortly after the Germans arrived in Austria, they began to arrest people who supported any political party (other than the Nazis), as well as prominent journalists, financiers, civil servants, and Jews. Emil knew he had to try to escape. He was especially in trouble because not only was he Jewish but he was also a Social Democrat, which was an anti-fascist party. He was briefly imprisoned, but when he was released he was given forty-eight hours to leave the country. He managed to escape to Belgium, along with

Marion's sixteen-year-old sister, Annie. At the time, lots of people were trying to escape and he probably thought that two people could get away more easily than four.

Marion's mother, Jetty, was more realistic about the situation than Emil had been. She said, "This is a fact. This is what we're facing. We have to stick together and overcome."[21] Emil soon sent a message to Jetty to travel to Cologne, Germany, where they were supposed to meet someone who would guide them to Belgium. The person never showed up, so Jetty and Marion had to return to Vienna.

A few months later, Emil sent another message to ask Jetty to try again to reach Belgium with Marion. On the way, they stopped in Munich, Germany. It was the fateful date of November 9, 1938—*Kristallnacht*, the "Night of Broken Glass." Marion saw how people were being "pushed and shoved and mishandled"; how the trains were crowded with people fleeing wherever they could. Marion's family would later learn that during those two days and nights, more than 1,000 synagogues in Germany were burned down. Rioters ransacked and looted about 7,500 Jewish businesses, killed at least 91 Jews, and vandalized Jewish hospitals, homes, schools, and cemeteries. How relieved Marion and Jetty must have felt when they met their guide, managed to enter Belgium, and were finally reunited with Emil and Annie!

Unfortunately, their haven in Belgium was to be short-lived. The Germans invaded Belgium in 1940, Emil was drafted into the Belgian army, and Jetty and the girls decided they had to flee to France. This was no easy task because the rail lines had been bombed. Jetty and her daughters spent fifteen days traveling between railway stations until at last they were able to enter France.

However, when they arrived in August 1940, they were considered "enemy aliens." They were sent to Gurs, an internment camp along France's southern border in the Pyrenees. The conditions in Gurs were terrible. Marion recalls,

"They didn't try to kill us; they tried to starve us to death."[22] Marion and her family, along with other prisoners, were forced to live in windowless, crowded cabins made of thin planks of wood, with tar paper roofs that leaked. The prisoners slept on sacks of straw on the floor. Food was scarce and poor in quality. There was no sanitation, running water, or plumbing. With frequent rain, the camp's paths were often like a sea of mud. Many people died of diseases like typhus and dysentery. Marion herself became very ill but somehow survived. She lived in Gurs with her mother and sister for almost one year.

Finally in May 1941, Annie persuaded Jetty that they had to leave the camp. Annie charmed the guards and Jetty bribed a guard by selling some jewelry she had hidden. They even managed to find Emil (through the Red Cross) and arranged his escape from his internment camp in Saint-Cyprien, a town on the coast of southern France.

The family finally made it to Marseille, the French city on the Mediterranean. It was just in time. If they had stayed after August, they most likely would have been sent to their deaths in Auschwitz. Jetty's aim was to go to Basel, Switzerland, where she had first cousins who were Swiss citizens.

During their nerve-wracking wait in Marseille, they stayed in a small apartment in the home of Silvio Pes, an Italian carpenter and his wife, Armida. As Marion's sister, Annie, later recalled, "Our situation wasn't very rosy. We had practically no money, not much expectation to make any and no place to go. So we lived from day to day, not knowing what the next morning would bring."[23]

In August 1942, when the police came looking for Jews, Silvio put a large padlock on the door of the hiding place to make the police think no one was there. He told them, "I don't have the key. It's an old rusty lock. It's always been there. I guarantee you that no one is behind the door."[24] While the police knocked on the door, Annie later recalled, "It seemed to us to go on for hours while we were afraid to breathe…. At last the lights and sounds stopped—still we did not move—luckily. Dawn came and we were still huddled together, frozen with fear."[25] Silvio finally came to tell them that the police had gone but that they would return. Now the family knew they could wait no longer to try to escape. (Years later, Marion's son Elisha Wiesel nominated Silvio and Armida Pes to be included in the Righteous Among the Nations—non-Jews who took great risks to save Jews during the Holocaust—at Yad Vashem, Israel. The Pes couple's names were put on the Wall of Honor in August 2020.)

After a month of hiding in a farmer's hut, in September 1942 the family managed to escape to Switzerland. "It was a hard long way," Annie later wrote, "and we spent many hours in fear."[26] Marion remembers having to walk down a dark tunnel with searchlights on both ends, and how her feet got wet from the grass. "Many people," she recalled, "were sent back, but because my aunt and cousins were citizens, we were allowed to enter Switzerland."[27]

Safe at last, during her time in Basel, Marion went to a girls "gymnasium" (high school) where she studied Hebrew, Bible, and other subjects. She also loved watching American movies and admired Hollywood stars like Shirley Temple, Cary Grant, and Bette Davis. In fact, that's how she began to learn English!

When World War II ended in 1945, the family set their sights on going to the United States. But it was no easy matter to get there. First, they had to go to Antwerp, Belgium, where they waited for their visas. Marion wanted to continue learning French, so every day she took a one-hour train ride to Brussels to study at a school there.

◊

Marion and her family finally arrived in New York City in 1949. They began a new life. Emil opened a furniture store in the Bronx. "New Life for Your Old Furniture" read one of their advertisements. However, the war had left an indelible mark on Marion. She had the feeling that she was "always in transit. Nothing is forever. Nothing is going to last."[28]

But Marion refused to think of herself as a victim. On the contrary, she felt she had won a victory over her Nazi oppressors. She threw herself into becoming "Americanized." She took courses at various colleges in Florida, and then came back to New York where she got a job at Russeks Department Store on Fifth Avenue. She met and married F. Peter Rose and they had a daughter, Jennifer.

The family lived a quiet life, similar to that of many other people around them, but something kept nagging at Marion. She was appalled to learn that racism existed in the United States. She felt it was similar to the prejudice she had lived through as her family fled from one country to another in Europe during the war. She felt both angry and afraid and was determined to do something about the injustices she saw. In the 1960s, Marion became a member of the National Association for the Advancement of Colored People (NAACP) to fight for civil rights and social justice.

Not only did Marion join the NAACP, but she participated in its activities. For example, while she lived in Florida, she tried several times to give her seat on the bus to an older Black person—even though she knew that most white people in that state disapproved of what she was doing. Marion didn't stop there. She made a practice of phoning for hotel reservations under a name that sounded "white." When she would arrive at the hotel with an African American friend, Marion and the Black man would find their reservation had been "lost."[29] She cherishes her NAACP membership card to this day.

In the late 1960s, Marion was in the process of divorcing her husband. Then she met journalist and professor Elie Wiesel. He describes their first meeting: "I wasn't sure what I found most striking about her: the delicacy of her features, the brilliance of her words, or the breadth of her knowledge of art, music, and the theater."[30] Her daughter, Jennifer Rose, says, "I watched my mother bloom into a person who wanted to…help others who…didn't have a voice."[31] Meeting Elie was a turning point in Marion's life, for their relationship gave her an opportunity to develop her potential.

Marion and Elie had a quiet wedding in Jerusalem in the spring of 1969, just before Passover. They were both overjoyed when their son, Elisha, was born on June 6, 1972. When Elisha was young, Elie and Marion would walk him to the yellow school bus that would take him to school. They both were devoted, careful parents, always marveling about the miracle that was their son.

During their years together, Elie worked tirelessly to write, speak, and educate people about the Holocaust. Marion often translated his work and helped him as he wrote important speeches. So, in 1979, President Jimmy Carter asked them both about their vision for a U.S. Holocaust Museum. As Tom Bernstein, former chair of the U.S. Holocaust Memorial Museum remarked, "They both said it had to be a teaching institution; history and memory had to inspire reflection, education, and ultimately, action."[32]

Marion began to work against racism in another way. In 1984, "Operation Moses" airlifted about 8,000 Ethiopian Jews to Israel so they could escape the social and economic persecution they faced at home. A few years later, Marion was visiting an Israeli friend in a little village in Israel when she saw the dire conditions these Ethiopian Jews were living in. She decided to try to help them as much as she could. She had seen examples of racism in the United States, and she was determined that that wouldn't happen in the new State of Israel.

In 1986, Elie received the Nobel Peace Prize. The committee stated that he was "a messenger to mankind: his message is one of peace, atonement and dignity."[33] Soon afterwards, their friend French President François Mitterrand asked them what they were planning to do with the sizeable prize money. At first, Elie and Marion weren't certain, but soon they created the Elie Wiesel Foundation for Humanity. As Marion recalls, "We had to do something important."[34] The couple then had to decide how best to use the funds available.

One special focus of Marion's work thus became the two Beit Tzipora Centers in Israel. (These centers are named after Elie's seven-year-old sister, Tzipora. She was killed in Auschwitz along with their mother, Sarah, in 1944.) Founded in 1986 in Ashkelon and Kiryat Malachi, the Centers focus on educating the Ethiopian-Jewish community and giving these students greater opportunities. Close to 1,000 boys and girls are currently enrolled in after-school programs. It's important to note that Marion not only provides funds from the Foundation for these schools, but for many years she visited them regularly to offer them hope and encouragement.

Elie was a brilliant speaker and writer, and Marion was always at his side. She was Elie's adviser and confidante, helping with all his important speeches. Fluent in five languages, she also translated fourteen of Elie's books from French to English—most recently, a new edition of *Night*, the first part of his memoir trilogy about the Holocaust. She has also produced many television programs, including *A Passover Haggadah*, *The World of Elie Wiesel*, and *The Oslo Concert: A Tribute to Peace*. In addition, she wrote and narrated the 1999 documentary film *Children of the Night*, which told the harrowing story of Jewish children in the ghettos and concentration camps during World War II.

In the dedication to his memoir, *All Rivers Run to the Sea*, Elie Wiesel wrote: "For almost thirty years, Marion Wiesel has been the first to read and edit the English versions of my books (when not translating them herself), including this volume of memoirs. I owe her more than gratitude."

Fitting words for a remarkable woman.

RITA ARDITTI

1934–2009

BUENOS AIRES, ARGENTINA, 1993

Rita felt a knot in her stomach as she rode up in the iron cage of the elevator to the fourth floor. She walked along the dark hall to the office where the Grandmothers organized their work. It was the first time she would meet them. When the door opened, she came face-to-face with photos of hundreds of children and their parents who had "disappeared."[35]

Rita Arditti was born in Buenos Aires, Argentina, on September 9, 1934. Her parents, Jacques Arditti and Rosa Cordovero, had immigrated separately to Argentina from Turkey in the early 1900s. They met and married and had three daughters—Edith, Rita, and Alicia. Rita's childhood was a happy one, for her father was a successful businessman and her mother took care of their home and the children. They led a comfortable, middle-class life. The three sisters, along with three female cousins, spent a lot of time together, visiting each other's houses and going to movies on the weekends.

But life wasn't always easy for Sephardic Jews in Argentina. Most of the Jewish people there had originally come from Eastern Europe, so were from an Ashkenazic background. The Sephardic Jews had originally lived in Spain or Portugal and, after they were expelled in 1492, had settled in many other countries, especially those around the Mediterranean Sea. Because the Sephardic Jews were a "minority within a minority," they often weren't accepted into the larger Jewish community, let alone the Argentinian community.

When Rita was a girl, she was often mistaken for a Catholic because of her Italian-sounding name. She would sometimes hear antisemitic remarks about Jews because people thought she would go along with their comments. For the rest of her life, she always made sure to tell people she was Jewish, and she never hesitated to stand up for anyone who was being persecuted, Jew or non-Jew. This attitude prompted her to eventually become a human rights activist.

When Rita was completing elementary school, she found out about a bilingual, Spanish-English private high school called El Colegio Ward. It sounded to Rita like a very good school—better than the one in her own neighborhood. Since her father was always supportive of Rita's education, he agreed to let her go. The school had high standards and prepared her for her future studies. Rita loved the academic challenge, but it wasn't an easy time. For the first three years, Rita boarded at the school during the week and, during her senior year, she commuted an hour and a half each way.

Not only did Rita work hard at school but she also studied piano. She was so proficient that, at the age of seventeen, she played a Bach concerto with the Buenos Aires Radio Symphony. Rita was rather shy and didn't like the pressure leading up to a performance. So, she decided not to become a concert pianist even though her teacher encouraged her to do so. However, she played piano for her own pleasure for the rest of her life.

Because Rita's grades were so high, she was admitted to Barnard College in New York City. She had heard about this women's college and wanted to leave home to study abroad. Even then, Rita had a rebellious streak!

She wasn't happy at Barnard because most of the other students in the dormitory were much older than she was. However, during her time there, she met Mario Muchnik, a fellow Argentinian. They started dating and returned to Argentina, but then decided to study in Italy together. Their decision to leave the country was probably because Argentina was going through a lot of political and economic upheavals at the time, and they were worried they might not be able to continue their studies.

She and Mario both enrolled at the University of Rome—Rita in biology and Mario in physics. They got married in 1955 and had a son, Federico, in 1960. After Rita completed her doctorate the following year, she started to do research in genetics in a laboratory in Naples. Meanwhile, the couple realized that they had different ambitions. Rita wanted to continue her work in science—this time, in the U.S.—and not be restricted to the role of wife and mother; Mario stayed in Italy and eventually became a publisher. Rita and Mario separated and divorced; however, they stayed friends for the rest of Rita's life.

In 1965, Rita and Federico moved to Boston, along with Paolo Strigini, Rita's first true love. As Federico recalls, Paolo was a great stepdad. Paolo taught him how to ride a bike, walked him to school, and "flew him" to bed.[36]

However, after about ten years, Rita and Paolo separated. Rita continued studying biology as a postdoctoral fellow at Brandeis University. A year later, she was hired by Dr. Jonathan Beckwith to work in his lab in the department of bacteriology and immunology at Harvard University Medical School.

All her experiences made Rita aware that most of the top positions in science were held by men. Well-educated women like herself were stuck on the lower rungs of the academic ladder. In 1970, she and a group of women published a pamphlet, *How Harvard Rules Women*. Working on the pamphlet with like-minded women heightened Rita's awareness of the gender gap in work and education. That pamphlet was the beginning of Rita's feminist activities.

A year later, Rita began to teach about science and society at Boston University. During that period, she helped to found an organization called Science for the People. It aimed to educate people about the politics and the sometimes negative uses of science. She wrote articles for the group's magazine until the late 1980s.

Rita's energy and her passion propelled her to juggle several jobs at the same time. Often, when she was concerned about an issue, she wrote an article or book about it. For instance, she was worried about the new reproductive technologies, like in vitro fertilization, and the impact they would have on women. Her research into these reproductive technologies led her to edit (and write an article in) a book called *Test-Tube Women* that was first published in 1984. In the book, she asks, "Why is it that men are so interested in tampering with women's reproductive biology?"[37] Some of the questions she raised over fifty years ago are still relevant today.

In 1974, she and three other women—Gilda Bruckman, Mary Lowry, and Jean MacRae—talked about the need for a safe place where people interested in women's issues could buy feminist books and magazines and where they could meet and discuss their concerns. The group weren't just talkers; they were doers. They opened a cooperative bookstore called New Words Bookstore. Together, with pooled funds of $15,000, they created one of the first women's spaces in the Boston area. They shared the work, the profits, and the headaches!

Rita's life wasn't filled only with work and activism. She made time to travel with Federico and have fun. They often went for pizza at Regina Pizzeria across the river in Boston. They traveled to Disney World; another time, to San Juan, Puerto Rico. They also visited Rita's family in Buenos Aires—sisters, cousins, her mother Rosa, and many friends. Once, Rita even bought a used red Mercedes-Benz convertible![38]

In 1974, Rita was confronted with many challenges: While beginning a very demanding job teaching an interdisciplinary doctoral program, she was diagnosed with breast cancer. That diagnosis meant that she had to have a breast removed. She was only thirty-nine years old. She wondered how she would cope with all these changes. How could she be strong for herself and for Federico, who was only fourteen years old at the time? Could she continue to work and support the causes that were important to her? Because she was Rita, she could, and she did!

In 1980, Rita's life changed yet again. A few years had passed since she had separated from Paolo, but then she met Estelle Disch, the woman who would be her partner for the next twenty-nine years. When they met, Estelle was a professor of sociology as well as an artist. They were both attending a workshop about exploring alternative treatments for illness. They had a lot in common: physical intimacy, books, friends, and causes they believed in.

In 1991, Rita co-founded the Women's Community Cancer Project (WCCP), which focused both on women's issues and on the environmental causes of cancer. Although Rita was shy, when she cared about a cause, she could put aside her shyness and speak in public. As Estelle described her, "Rita never wanted attention but attention sought her out."[39]

As well as human rights issues, Rita began to explore her Sephardic Jewish identity. Rita was a voracious reader and, after reading more about Sephardic history, she decided that she wanted to educate people about her heritage. Being Rita, she wrote an article about being Sephardic that was published in an anthology about Jewish women.[40] As part of her investigations, in 1999 she and Estelle took a trip to Turkey, where Rita's parents came from. Rita even found the house in Izmir where her mother had grown up.

Another important focus of Rita's life occurred in 1986 when she found out that hundreds of babies and children had been kidnapped in Argentina during what was known as "the Dirty War," which took place from 1977 to 1983. It was a time when her homeland was taken over by a military dicta-torship; when thousands of young people were arrested, tortured, and usually "disappeared." What really happened is that they were killed, often in brutal ways.

Rita soon learned about a group of grandmothers, *abuelas* in Spanish, who were looking for their "disappeared" children and grandchildren. Every Thursday, these grandmothers, wearing white headscarves, marched in a circle in the main central plaza in Buenos Aires. During a series of trips to Argentina, Rita befriended the *abuelas* and gained their trust.

In 1993, she began interviewing them about their experiences. As usu-al, her activism turned into writing. She researched and wrote the book, *Searching for Life: The Grandmothers of the Plaza de Mayo and the Disappeared Children of Argentina*. It was the first English book about the grandmothers, and it brought the attention of the world to this tragic situation. Of the many projects and causes that Rita supported, she was most proud of her work with the *abuelas*.

Rita passed away on December 25, 2009, at the age of 75. For most of her life, Rita felt like an outsider—a Sephardic Jew in Argentina, a woman scientist, a cancer patient. But Rita often said, "Feel the fear and do it anyway."[41] She marched for, spoke about, and donated to many causes, like Native American rights, the NAACP, and women's rights—not only in the United States and Argentina, but also around the world.

During a tribute program for Rita in 2012, Lisa Baldez said, "Rita was shorter than I am, but always seemed so tall."[42] Rita Arditti's work will never be lost. It will continue to inspire young people to work for women's equality and social justice now and in the future.

MARIKA GIDALI

1937–

BUDAPEST, HUNGARY, 1944

Marika and her older sister, Agnes, cowered in the dank basement. Above them, they could hear the heavy boots of German soldiers looking for Jews. Where were Mama and Papa? The sisters were alone, with no one to help them. Marika shivered. Would she ever see her parents again? Would she ever be free again?

Marika Gidali was born in Budapest on April 29, 1937.[43] Her father, Bela (Benjamin) Gidali, was a tailor and her mother, Elizabeth, was a seamstress from a poor family in Budapest. After the couple married, they sewed clothes for both men and women in their cozy apartment.

Marika recalls, "my grandfather, who was called Gabor, lived with us. I loved going to his room. As a matter of fact, it was on the sofa in my grandfather's bedroom that I started doing acrobatics."[44] Gabor was her mother's father and a widower, so he was a welcome part of the close-knit family. They practiced Judaism, especially during the High Holidays, and Bela often spoke about Judaism around the dinner table.[45]

The situation for Jews was very hard in the 1930s when Marika was growing up. It was difficult to make a living and even to travel around the city. Jews were forced to wear the Jewish star on the front of their clothes whenever they went outside. They were often bullied and harassed when they went to buy food or go to work or school. Marika remembers how non-Jews had priority on the sidewalk and she would have to walk on the road to let them pass.[46]

Things went from bad to worse. Beginning in 1938, Hungary's leaders began to enact anti-Jewish laws like those in Nazi Germany. So Bela and Elizabeth decided to have Marika and her older sister, Agnes, baptized. They thought the girls would be safer if they were Christians.

In 1941, Hungary allied itself with the "Axis" powers of Germany, Italy, and Japan. Soon afterwards, Marika's father was sent to the front line of the battle between Germany and the Soviet Union. Marika recalls, "The Jews always were the first ones to be taken to the front…. I was only a child and I didn't understand much of what was going on."[47] Bela was stationed in Komárom, Hungary, where he did hard labor loading cannonballs. He was eventually captured by the Soviet army and sent as a prisoner of war to the concentration camp of Bergen-Belsen, from which he was released at the end of the war.

Meanwhile, Marika's mother, aunt, two cousins, and Marika and Agnes stayed together in their apartment. One time during those fearful months, they were all rounded up along with other Jews in the neighborhood and forced to walk to the soccer stadium, miles away from their home. The whole time, Marika had to keep her aching arms raised up as the soldiers pointed their rifles at the Jews plodding along the road. After a terrifying night in the stadium, they were (for some unknown reason) allowed to go home.

Another time, Marika's mother and aunt were forced to go to the stadium again—this time, without the children. Where they were, the girls didn't know. What Marika did know was that she and the other girls had to hide. First, they found shelter in a Red Cross orphanage on the same street as theirs. "The bombings increased when we were in the orphanage," Marika remembers. "Either we were doing nothing at all in our rooms, or we were running to the basement to protect ourselves from the bombs."[48] What's more, because of the lack of good food, Marika developed open sores on her body and inside her mouth.

Later, when Marika's mother returned, they all moved to the ghetto across the river in Pest. Elizabeth was not allowed to keep her daughters with her, so she took them to a children's home. The place was crowded and the children had little food, but they managed to stay there until the end of the war.

Meanwhile, in March 1944, just one month before Marika's seventh birthday, German tanks rolled into Hungary. The Nazis were impatient with the slowness of the Hungarian government to send its Jews to their deaths; so, Germany decided to take things into its own hands. Marika didn't know it then, but between May 15 and July 9, over 400,000 Jews were deported from Hungary to the infamous concentration camp of Auschwitz. Most of them were murdered when they arrived.

Finally, in January and February of 1945, the invading Soviet army freed Budapest from the Nazis. Marika remembers, "the Russians came into the city from underground and when they emerged, they threw chocolate and lots of things for us."[49]

Marika and her sister were miraculously reunited with their parents. Marika's younger brother, Peter Pal (Pedro), was born in 1946 shortly after the war ended.

They were free, but still had many hurdles to overcome. Bela and Elizabeth wanted to leave Hungary. Their memories of the country were painful and they were afraid that life would be dangerous again under the Soviets.

But where could they go? Elizabeth's sister, Lena, had gone to Brazil years before, so they aimed to go there. But Brazil had shut its gates to Jews and the family couldn't get permission to enter the country.

Bela managed to get false papers for the family to go to Brazil, but when they arrived at the port of Santos, they weren't allowed to land. They then decided to go to neighboring Uruguay and, two weeks later, were smuggled across the border. Finally in 1947, they arrived in the city of São Paulo.

◊

Marika loved living in her new country. She could walk down the street without anyone telling her she had to cross to the other side or walk on the road, and without anyone spitting at her or beating her up. But it was hard to be an immigrant in this new country. As Marika recalls, "I didn't speak Portuguese, and I did not know anyone in the country.... School was really challenging because I didn't speak the language and I didn't understand the teachers.... I had no friends and no one to talk to or to help me."[50]

However, Marika was lucky because she found a way to feel better about her situation. When she was young, she had taught herself to dance and do acrobatics by watching movies. These skills led to her dancing short pieces at the local Hungarian Club, where she also took part in small theater productions.

When she was sixteen years old, she left school and joined the Ballet of the Fourth Centenary, a company founded in that year by Hungarian choreographer Aurélio Miloss. Three years later when the company was disbanded, Marika moved to Rio de Janeiro and joined the ballet company of Theatro Municipal, where she danced in ballets created by international choreographers.

Marika realized that she didn't have a "perfect ballet body." She said, "I suffered because I didn't have the ideal physique, that is: long legs, a straight back, a long neck, curved feet. I didn't have any of these."[51] But she worked very hard and mastered the difficult ballet technique.

In 1957, when Marika was twenty years old, she returned to São Paulo and joined various ballet companies, but each one folded after only a short time. In 1965, Marika traveled to Germany and danced in the Cologne International Festival. Soon afterwards, she was invited to join the Cologne Opera Company. However, Marika wanted to return to Brazil, for she felt she could make more of a difference there than in Europe.

When Marika returned to São Paulo, she opened a ballet school on Sarandí Street. The school became the meeting place for both dancers and actors. Marika next started a dance group called *Afirmação* (Affirmation). Through her work at the school and interactions with other artists, Marika was discovering how to blend theater and dance together, leading her to create a number of important works for the stage and television.

In 1964, a military dictatorship led by the army, with the support of the Catholic Church and anti-communist groups, had taken over the government. The dictatorship stifled freedom of speech and political opposition. Hundreds of people were killed; thousands were imprisoned. The dictatorship lasted until 1985.

During that time, Marika decided to use dance to express her opposition to the dictatorship. This was a great act of courage because the government punished anyone who spoke against it. Marika recalls, "Everything the dictatorship tried to prohibit, we dared to disobey. Everything we were not allowed to say, we said through dance."[52]

During that terrifying time, Marika decided that she had to suppress her memories of wartime Hungary and the Holocaust. She says, "I shut those memories out, buried them in concrete. I did not keep bad feelings about it. I preferred not to stop and suffer or grieve, but to keep moving forward."[53] Marika didn't want to be filled with bitterness and resentment; she always wanted to keep progressing in her life and her work.

In 1971, Marika married the dancer Décio Otero, with whom she produced the television series *Invitation to Dance* for Culture Television in São Paulo. In that same year, Marika and Décio founded their company, Ballet Stagium. This company was unique in Brazil and Latin America, for its dance works reflected Brazilian life and society.

But Marika and Décio weren't satisfied performing only for audiences in São Paulo. They took their dances all around Brazil, including into areas where Indigenous people lived—people who had never seen their kind of dance before. Marika says, "It was a turning point in our minds as we saw our dance was not 'superior,' but just another dance. I was just another person who goes to center stage to communicate. We were neither more, nor less, than each other."[54]

Because Marika remembered how she had suffered as a child, she was determined to bring dance to people and places that were not the "norm"—public schoolyards, slums, prisons, cinemas, town squares, hospitals, churches, subway stations, and parades. The company's pieces frequently dealt with diffi-cult social issues like violence, racism, the environment, AIDS, and genocide. For example, in 1985, Marika performed the ballet *Crimes*, choreographed by Décio and set in a concentration camp. Ballet Stagium has also developed educational programs inside juvenile detention centers and SOS Children's Villages, where orphaned and abandoned children are cared for. Dance was no longer for the rich and privileged, but for people everywhere.

As Marika says, "I'm always walking on a tightrope. I'm strong enough to walk on it. My childhood led me to a country where I can do something good for society."[55]

JUDY FELD CARR

1938–

SUDBURY, CANADA, 1945

Judy Leve was taking the shortcut home from school. Suddenly, a group of five or six older kids surrounded her. They began calling her, "Dirty Jew!" and throwing rocks at her. Judy ran home crying. Her face was dirty, her lips were cut and swollen, and her front teeth had been knocked out. That night at the Passover seder, Judy had to eat chicken soup through a straw. She never forgave the kids who had bullied her.[56]

Judy Feld Carr was born in Montreal on December 26, 1938, to Jack Leve, her Russian-born father, and Sarah (née Rives), who had been raised in Brooklyn, New York. They met at a wedding in Montreal and after they were married, lived in Montreal for a few years. When Judy was five years old, one year after her brother Alexander was born, Jack Leve decided to move the family to Sudbury. He was a fur trapper and trader, and needed to be closer to his work.

In the 1940s, Sudbury was a small town in northern Ontario, with a population of fewer than 2,000 people. When the Leve family moved there, the main industries were logging and nickel mining. Judy remembers Sudbury as an "ugly, small, dark town; where the soot from the chimneys turned the snow black."[57]

Jack traded furs with Indigenous trappers, so he often had to be on the road or in the bush for long periods of time. While he was away, Judy's mother and grandmother took care of the children. The Jewish community in Sudbury and other towns in northern Ontario was small—consisting of only about thirty families—but Judy's mother was involved with a Jewish women's group called Hadassah and she made some close friends. At the same time, Judy made friends with Jewish children from the other small towns nearby.

While Judy was growing up in Sudbury, she often had to face antisemitism; she was called names and even beaten up. Her father stood up for Judy with the school principal and teachers whenever she was bullied. He also taught her how to fight, to shoot a gun, to paddle a canoe, and to catch and fillet fish. Judy decided she would work hard at school, get good grades, and show her teachers and fellow students that she could succeed, in spite of their insults.[58]

Many years later, after Judy's secret work smuggling Jews out of Syria became known, Itzhak Shelef, the former Israeli ambassador to Canada, said, "I believe her childhood molded her. Anyone who's been to her region, especially in the days of her childhood, knows it was a tough place to live in and especially to grow up in as a girl."[59]

Two important events happened when Judy was about eight years old. World War II was over by then and people were just beginning to find out about what would be called the "Holocaust." Over six million Jews were killed in Europe—for no reason except that they were Jews.

One day, Judy was playing on the floor in her parents' bedroom while Jack was rearranging his dresser drawers. Without thinking, he placed a pile of newspaper clippings on the floor next to Judy. She began to look through them. Although she couldn't understand a lot of the details, she was horrified to see pictures of starving people and of mass graves. She asked her father, "What's that?" but he shooed her away. He didn't want to talk about it.

Shortly afterwards, the Leve family heard a knock on the door. The woman standing there had seen the Simchat Torah flags that Judy's brother, Alex, had taped to his window to mark the Jewish holiday. She pointed to the *mezuzah* on the doorpost and timidly asked in Yiddish, "Is this a Jewish home?" When she was reassured that it was, indeed, a Jewish home, the woman said her name was Sophie. She was invited inside.

After that beginning, Sophie often came over to the Leve home. She was warmly welcomed and became like part of the family. One night, she began to speak about herself. She told the Leve family about how she had been married before the war and had two children. Her husband and children had been killed in Auschwitz, the concentration camp, while Sophie had had horrific experiences there.

She treated Judy like a daughter and Judy became very attached to her, like a "surrogate mother."[60] In 1956, when Judy finished high school and left Sudbury to study music at the University of Toronto, she promised Sophie that she would always do her best to make sure that Jews never again suffered as Sophie had.[61] That promise began a lifelong commitment.

During Judy's third year at university, she met Ronald (Rubin) Feld, who had grown up in a poor family in downtown Toronto. He had worked his way through medical school, all the while supporting his widowed mother and his younger sister. Judy and Ronald had a whirlwind romance, got married in 1960, spent their honeymoon in Israel, and settled in Toronto.

The 1960s was a time of political discontent in the United States. The movement to gain civil rights for Black people was going strong, as well as protests against the Vietnam War. Many people in Canada were also involved in these movements and other social justice reforms. Judy and Ronald became aware of the plight of Jews who were not allowed to leave the Soviet Union or Syria, even though their lives were being threatened. While lots of people were advocating for the Soviet Jews, Judy and Ronald decided they would try to help the Syrian Jews, for few people seemed interested or able to help them.

Why were the Syrian Jews in trouble? After 1947, when the United Nations created the State of Israel, the life of Jews living in Arab lands, such as in North Africa, in Tunisia, Morocco, and Algeria, became increasingly difficult. Many Jews were beaten up and even murdered; Jewish homes and businesses were looted; Jewish schools and synagogues were closed down. Jews were often left penniless and were desperate to seek a safe place to live. Thousands of Jews left those countries and settled in Israel or other countries. About five thousand Jews remained in Syria and couldn't get out.

After the Six-Day War in 1967, when Israel repulsed attacks from Jordan, Syria, and Egypt and gained territory in the Golan Heights, East Jerusalem, and the West Bank, the situation became even more difficult for Syrian Jews. They had to endure all kinds of new rules and regulations. For example, there were limits on buying or selling property, operating a car, or even getting a telephone. Mail was censored and telephone calls were monitored by the *Mukhabarat*, the secret police that everyone feared. People who were caught trying to escape illegally were thrown into prison and tortured. The prisoners could not get justice from the courts.

Starting in 1971, Judy and Ronald tried to help the Jews of Syria. Judy explains: "We decided to call someone in Damascus. Who in Damascus, we don't know. Maybe the whole thing was *meshugah* (crazy). What were we doing? We don't know what we're doing."[62] They held onto a slim thread of hope when, in the winter of 1972, they and Toronto Rabbi Serels managed (after three weeks and many attempts) to speak to Rabbi Hamra in Damascus. After that phone call, further communication was done through telegrams and letters because they worried their calls would be monitored by the Syrian secret police.

Judy and Ronald subsequently sent two parcels to the Jewish community in Damascus—one containing books; the other, religious articles like prayer shawls. Several coded messages of "greeting" were also placed in the boxes. However, by 1973, after not getting much help from the Canadian government or the Canadian Jewish Congress, the Felds decided that they had to do something more, in secret, and on their own. But things did not go according to plan.

After Judy and Ronald returned from a trip to Israel in May 1973, Ronald was playing with his youngest child when he had a heart attack and suddenly died. He was only forty years old.

Because his death was so unexpected, Judy had to figure out a way to earn a living and to support her three young children. She fell back on her music training. She got a job teaching high school music during the day and giving private piano lessons in the evening.

Judy could have given up the campaign on behalf of the Syrian Jews. She could have backed away and settled into her own private life. But Judy was a fighter. She remembered how important it was to free the Jews of Syria. She remembered how she had promised Sophie back in Sudbury that she would help Jews who were suffering.

At first, however, she could do very little. As historian Harold Troper wrote, "She could scarcely make ends meet or find time for herself and her children."[63] However, a few weeks after Ronald's death, a group of friends from the Beth Tzedec synagogue in Toronto met at Judy's home. After some discussion, they proposed that the Dr. Ronald Feld Fund be established to collect money to help the Syrian Jews. Five thousand dollars was pledged then and there. Everyone assumed that Judy would administer these funds donated from people across Canada and the United States. Judy still wasn't sure she could manage this task, but she knew she had to try.

A few years after Ronald's death, Judy met Donald Carr, a lawyer and a prominent member of the Canadian Jewish community. He was a widower with three children of his own. Judy and Donald were married in 1977. Now Judy was both working and running a home with a blended family: her three children, Alan, Gary, and Elizabeth and Donald's three children, Aaron, Jonathan, and Adam.

At first, Judy's work was only to send religious books to the Jewish communities in Syria. But then came a turning point. She received a hand-delivered letter from three rabbis in Aleppo saying, "Please get us out…. Our children are your children."[64] In 1980, Judy heard that a Jewish man had been able to "buy" his way out of Syria. She thought that, if one person was able to escape that way, then perhaps many more could. Troper writes, "The possibility to rescue Jews from Syria excited her, and she was not going to let any opportunity slip through her fingers."[65]

Judy decided to become a rescuer. Step by careful step, she set up an underground network in order to send money into Syria and thus bribe officials to allow Jews to leave—to go wherever they could find a safe haven. Judy's work changed from sending books and religious objects *into* Syria to getting people *out*.

She arranged with smugglers to take some Syrian Jews over the heavily guarded border to Turkey, but that method was extremely dangerous. If they were caught, they would be imprisoned and probably tortured.

Judy preferred to "pay off" officials to allow Jews out of the country. This was no easy task. "Everyone involved, from clerks, government officials, and judges, to Mukhabarat agents had to be paid off," she explains.[66] By the 1980s, the number of people Judy was ransoming out of Syria climbed into the hundreds and then into the thousands.[67]

The people in Syria, the "operatives" who helped Judy, will probably never be known. In fact, they seldom knew one another. Furthermore, they didn't know who Judy was. As she says, "I was the best kept secret in the Jewish world."[68]

It was vital that every part of the operation was kept secret. At first, the *Mossad*, the Israeli secret service who were also working to help Syrian Jews escape, were suspicious of Judy. They probably wondered how a Canadian woman, a mother of six children, could be smuggling Jews out of Syria. Why was she doing it? Would she make a mistake and foil the whole operation? However, they gradually began to trust Judy; to give her information about individuals, escape routes, and even the weather. As Judy says, "I wasn't trained in foreign intrigue, but I could figure it out."[69]

During the course of over twenty-five years, Judy and her underground network rescued 3,228 Jews from Syria. Most of the people whom she brought out of Syria settled in Israel, New York City, or South America. The last family escaped from Syria on September 11, 2001. It was only when she received the Order of Canada in that year that Judy herself told her story.

In 1993, a group of Syrian Jewish leaders in New York proclaimed, "Judy Feld Carr has saved entire worlds and will be blessed by generations to come."[70] Judy still treasures a letter she received in 1995 from Yizhak Rabin, then prime minister of Israel: "Words cannot express my gratitude to you for 23 years of hard and dangerous work, during which you devoted your time and your life to the Jewish community in Syria."[71]

Why did Judy do what she did? When she was a young girl in Sudbury, she had learned to fight against bullies and antisemitism. She had made a promise to Sophie to help Jews in need. She made good on that promise.

ROSALIE SILBERMAN ABELLA

1946–

TORONTO, CANADA, 1950

"Tata, what's wrong?" four-year-old Rosalie asked as she went to meet her father at the door of their small apartment. Jacob Silberman's shoulders were slumped and his eyes were sad. He sat down and took her onto his lap. "The Canadian government will not allow me to practice law until I am a citizen. But I cannot wait so long." He stroked his daughter's hair. "Do not worry, little one. I will find another way to support our family." Rosalie put her hand into her father's hand. "Tata, when I grow up, I will be a lawyer too."

Rosalie Silberman's father, Jacob, was born in 1910 in Sienno, Poland to the son of a bookstore owner. When Jacob began university, he was one of only four Jews admitted that year. However, he eventually obtained his law degree from the prestigious Jagiellonian University in Kraków. That was an accomplishment truly remarkable for a Jew in 1930s antisemitic Poland.

Rosalie's mother, Fanny, was the daughter of a wealthy roofing supply manufacturer. She was born in 1917 in the town of Ostrowiec, Poland. Fanny and Jacob married on September 3, 1939—just as the Germans were invading Poland; just when World War II began.

Somehow, the couple managed to survive the six terrible years of war, although they could not stay together for most of the time. Fanny and her mother were imprisoned in various labor and concentration camps. In 1945, they were liberated from the Buchenwald concentration camp in Germany. Most of their families, even Fanny and Jacob's young son, were killed in Treblinka, a death camp in Poland.

Fanny never gave up hope that Jacob was alive. When she was finally freed, she and her mother went back to Ostrowiec where she and Jacob had lived before they were rounded up and imprisoned. She learned that Jacob was in Theresienstadt, near Prague. Somehow, in spite of all the chaos in the postwar period, she managed to travel to Czechoslovakia (now the Czech Republic). She learned that the people in the camp were quarantined because of a typhoid epidemic, but she sneaked in with a garbage detail anyway. She found Jacob, who was recovering from the illness, and managed to get him out of the camp. The couple spent a few days in Prague and then returned to Poland.

However, they soon realized it wasn't safe to stay in Poland because of the prevailing antisemitism and frequent attacks on surviving Jews. So, along with Fanny's mother, they made their way to a displaced persons (DP) camp in Stuttgart, Germany. They hoped they would eventually leave the camp and be able to find a new home in a different country.

Jacob became the president of the DP camp's Jewish Community Council. He even taught himself English when the Americans asked him to set up a system of legal services for displaced persons in southwest Germany.

Even though Jacob and Fanny mourned the loss of their home and their families, they were eager to start a new family. Rosalie was born in the DP camp on July 1, 1946, and her sister Toni was born there in 1948. Rosalie's first language was German although she spoke Yiddish to her grandmother.

Jacob tried for years to get visas for the family to enter Canada. It wasn't until 1950, when Rosalie was four years old, that they finally arrived in Toronto. They settled into an apartment on the third floor of a house in Toronto's Kensington Market. At that time, Jacob was forty years old, Fanny was thirty-three, and Rosalie's grandmother was over sixty.

Jacob wanted to practice law in Canada, but he was told he would have to wait five years until he became a citizen. Although he was bitterly disappointed, he knew he had to support his family. So, he became an insurance agent instead of a lawyer.

Rosalie learned something important from her father's experience. She later said, "When you are an immigrant, you never think in terms of entitlement. You think in terms of opportunities and working really hard."[72]

Rosalie's childhood was a busy one. She and her sister Toni went to the local public school near their home. They began piano lessons at school and later had more advanced lessons with a private teacher. After school on Friday afternoons, they went to the local public library to return their three allotted books and to take out three more. Every Saturday, they had ballet and tap dancing lessons. On Sunday mornings, the girls went to Shaarei Shomayim synagogue, where they learned about Jewish history and traditions.

By that time, the Silberman family had moved to the central Toronto area near Oakwood and St. Clair. There were few other Jewish children in their neighborhood, so Rosalie and Toni learned to make friends with everyone.

Although Rosalie's parents didn't dwell upon their experiences during the war, Rosalie came to understand what those experiences meant to them and how she herself was shaped by them. She later recalled, "I realized that what seemed so normal to me was in fact extraordinary, and that the real miracle was how people who had lived through what my parents had lived through could provide so normal a home."[73] She felt she had an obligation to repay her parents for the efforts they made to rebuild their lives.

Rosalie worked hard at her piano lessons and her schoolwork. By the time she was ten years old, she was known as a piano prodigy, winning many awards and appearing regularly on television, which in those days was a new sensation. She was one of the youngest graduates of the Royal Conservatory of Music, having earned a diploma in classical piano at age eighteen. She also graduated from high school with one of the highest grade averages in the province of Ontario.

Rosalie attended the University of Toronto (U of T), where she earned a BA in 1967. While she was there, she met her soon-to-be husband, Irving Abella, who became a noted Canadian historian. They got married in 1968, and their first son, Jacob, was born in 1973.

Rosalie's beloved father, Jacob, had passed away in 1970, just before Rosalie graduated from the U of T law school. Soon afterwards, she opened her own law practice where she accepted all kinds of cases—family, civil, and criminal.

In 1975, when Rosalie was only twenty-nine years old, she was appointed a judge in the Ontario Family Court. Some of her friends advised her not to take the position and told her that Family Court was a "dead end." They thought she should wait for better opportunities. But Rosalie didn't hesitate. She thought, "People like me—female, Jewish, immigrant, refugee—weren't exactly being appointed to the bench in droves.... After all, immigrants live for opportunities, not entitlements."[74]

Rosalie became Canada's first Jewish woman judge and the country's youngest ever, and she was pregnant as well! Zachary, their second son, was born that year. Perhaps she wondered how she would manage such a high-stress job along with the responsibilities of motherhood. She was always grateful that she had help from her mother and could also hire caregivers. Over the next seven years, sitting in her high seat in the courtroom, Rosalie learned to "look at people in front of you from their eyes and not from the top down."[75]

Becoming the first Jewish woman judge was the first of many milestones in Rosalie's long and illustrious career. She welcomed every opportunity that came her way. "It was *chutzpah* in full flight,"[76] she later said. While she was still in her twenties, Rosalie was appointed to various commissions and committees. In 1983, she wrote a ground-breaking study, *Access to Legal Services by the Disabled*, for the Ontario Ministry of the Attorney General. Before that time, most people weren't aware of the special legal needs that people with disabilities had. She called this "a new and difficult area of the law."[77]

In 1984, Rosalie was the one-person commissioner and author of the federal (Canadian) *Royal Commission on Equality in Employment*. She wanted to find ways to reduce barriers to employment that were faced by women, Indigenous people, visible minorities, and people with disabilities. She thought long and hard to develop a clear definition of "equality" and "discrimination." She came to the conclusion that the idea of equality means that you recognize differences and take them into account. Her report was used by the governments of Canada, New Zealand, Northern Ireland, and South Africa.

Rosalie was glad to know that her definition was used by the Supreme Court of Canada in its first equality decision. The Supreme Court ruled that a person could practice law even if he or she wasn't a Canadian citizen. Rosalie felt that an opportunity that had been denied to her father could from then on be given to other people.

A few years later, Rosalie became a visiting professor of law at McGill University in Montreal and at the University of Toronto. In March 1992, she became a judge on the Ontario Court of Appeal. One of her important judgements during that time had to do with the rights of gay couples. At that time, most people couldn't imagine that a same-sex couple should have the same rights as a heterosexual couple. Rosalie's landmark ruling said that "spouse" referred to the partner in a heterosexual *or* a homosexual couple. That decision meant that, if one spouse dies, the surviving spouse is entitled to the "survivor pension" from the government.

Rosalie's work has had a great impact in Canada and throughout the world. In addition to being a judge for more than forty-five years, she authored or co-authored four books and more than ninety journal articles. She's delivered hundreds of lectures all over the world and has been given thirty-nine honorary degrees from various universities.

Rosalie has had many "firsts" during her career: She was the first pregnant woman (and the youngest person ever) to be appointed to the bench in Canada, the first woman in the British Commonwealth to head a law reform commission, and the first woman to chair the Ontario Labour Relations Board. In yet another record-setting accomplishment, in 2004 Rosalie was appointed to the Supreme Court of Canada. She was thus the first Jewish woman appointed to the highest court of the land and, in fact, ended up being the longest-sitting justice on the Supreme Court.

She once said, "We will promise our children that we will do everything humanly possible to keep the world safer…a world where all children, regardless of race, color, religion, or gender can wear their identities with dignity, with pride, and in peace."[78]

Rosalie Silberman Abella has made a lasting contribution to the Jewish community, her adopted country of Canada, and to the world. When Rosalie was a little girl, she had promised her father she would become a lawyer. She met her parents' expectations, and much more.

PAULINE BEBE

1964–

PARIS, FRANCE, EARLY 1990s

Pauline was standing among the congregants of her synagogue after the Shabbat (Saturday) service when a man approached her. "Are you really a rabbi?" he said. Pauline took a big breath and answered, "Yes. I am." The man furrowed his brow. "Maybe you should grow a beard then." He walked away, laughing. It wasn't the first time that Pauline had heard that so-called joke. She knew it would not be the last.

Pauline Bebe was born in 1964, in Neuilly-sur-Seine, a suburb of Paris, France. Her parents, Eliane and Maurice, had a strong Jewish identity but hadn't had the opportunity when they were young to learn much about Judaism.

Pauline's mother, Eliane, was about eight years old in 1940 when Germany invaded France—part of its campaign to expand its territory during World War II. Eliane and her mother escaped from Paris to the south of France in order to get away from the Nazis. Millions of people from Belgium, the Netherlands, and France were also trying to find a safe place after their countries were overrun by Germany. It was called *l'Exode* or "the Exodus." Pauline's father, Maurice, and his brother were hidden by a Catholic family in southwest France. Most of his family were killed in the "Final Solution," the Nazi plan to kill all the Jews of Europe.

When Paris was finally liberated in August 1944, Maurice and Eliane returned to their city. They eventually met and married, but they had little chance to learn about Judaism while they were hiding from the Nazis. So, when Pauline and her older brother, Antoine, asked questions about antisemitism, for example, their parents had trouble answering their questions. Pauline's parents told her they would talk about antisemitism and the terrible things that had happened during the war, but they also wanted to tell her about the positive aspects of Judaism.[79]

Both Pauline's parents were strong role models, for each helped people in their own way. Maurice was a pediatrician and Eliane a lawyer. Maurice always slept with the phone by his bed so that, if a patient called, he would be ready to give them advice or even go to them.[80]

Pauline's parents decided to join the only liberal synagogue in Paris, situated on Rue Copernic. All the other synagogues in Paris at the time were "orthodox," following more traditional practices. For example, men and women sat separately during the services, and women could not read from the Torah or participate fully in many rituals. In that liberal synagogue, Pauline studied and prepared for her *bat mitzvah*, the coming-of-age ceremony for a Jewish girl, usually at twelve years old. Shortly afterwards, she began teaching children at the Talmud Torah, the religious school connected with the synagogue.

Pauline remembers coming home from school in the afternoon. A delicious snack, a *tartine*, would be waiting for her—a fresh baguette spread with butter and sprinkled with powdered chocolate along with a cup of hot chocolate. Often, Pauline brought a schoolmate home with her to share the treat. Even then, she realized that not everyone was as fortunate as she was.[81]

From the time she was young, Pauline's parents encouraged her to have an open mind and to explore possibilities in her life. Pauline said, "I was in a family which was enlightened and rational. They looked for a synagogue where there was equality between men and women."[82] Her parents believed that girls should be allowed to study the same subjects as boys. During her last year in high school, Pauline studied philosophy. By the time she finished university at the Institut National des Langues et Civilisations Orientales in Paris in 1985, she had obtained two degrees—one in English, the other in Hebrew.

However, by the time Pauline was eighteen years old, she had already decided she wanted to become a rabbi. When she told her parents about this goal, they were surprised and worried. They knew that most French Jews, who were Orthodox, would find the idea of a woman rabbi unacceptable. Nevertheless, her parents stood by Pauline as she continued her studies.

In 1985, Pauline enrolled at the Leo Baeck Rabbinical College in London, England—the only liberal Jewish college in Europe. During that time, she also studied for two years in Israel at three different institutions: Hebrew University in Jerusalem, Hebrew Union College, and Neve Schechter, the Conservative seminary. She remains good friends with fellow students she met during those years. She graduated from the Leo Baeck College in 1990, after which she worked at the West London Synagogue.

While in Israel, Pauline met her future husband, Tom Cohen, an American who was also studying to be a rabbi. The couple eventually moved to Paris, where Pauline was hired as the assistant rabbi of a synagogue. She thus made history by becoming the first female rabbi in France.

Pauline wanted a community where everyone was treated equally and welcomed openly. In 1995, she founded her own synagogue, La Communauté Juive Libérale d'Île-de-France (the Liberal Jewish Community of Ile-de-France). The following year, it changed its name to Maayan, meaning "the source." Maayan is part of the World Union of Progressive Judaism (le Judaïsme Libéral).

At first, some people were against the idea of a woman rabbi. However, after attending births (*brit milah* or baby namings), weddings, *bar* or *bat mitzvahs*, or burials, they often ended up saying, "Why *not* a woman rabbi?"[83]

To those who say that women should not be rabbis, Pauline answers, "Jewish law does not forbid a woman from being a rabbi because the question wasn't even asked before the movement of the equality of the sexes. Besides, many women in Jewish history held roles that a rabbi holds nowadays. Deborah was a judge in the Bible and Beruriah taught Jewish law in the Talmud."[84]

Pauline considers being a rabbi both a vocation and a passion.[85] She fulfills various roles as a rabbi, but she believes that teaching is the basis of her work. She prepares sermons that she hopes will touch the daily lives of her congregants and her students. She counsels people who have conflicts in their family or at work. She organizes conferences, debates, and artistic events.

Pauline and her congregants work regularly to further social justice: They help the sick and needy; welcome refugees; run clothing, food, and volunteer drives. She also helps people suffering from HIV/AIDS, people addicted to drugs, and parents who have lost children.

Pauline and her husband, Rabbi Tom Cohen, each have their own synagogue in different parts of Paris. However, they often work together. For example, they founded the first Reform Jewish camp in France called Camp MahaNetzer; they have Passover *seders* together; they share Judaism classes at both synagogues. They accomplish so much on top of raising their own four children!

Over the years, Pauline has written many books and articles. In 2001, she published *ISHA: Dictionnaire des Femmes et du Judaïsme (Dictionary of Women and Judaism)*. In 2003, she published the booklet, *Can We Make Our Children Happy?*; in the same year, she contributed to the journal *Revue Pardès* with the theme, "When Women Read the Bible." In 2006, she published her book, *What is Liberal Judaism?* and in 2013, *The Other: This Infinite Dialogue Around Love and Friendship*.

Pauline works with priests, imams, and other religious leaders to promote communication among various faiths; she often participates in interfaith dialogues and conferences. To further this goal, Pauline helped to create an annual one-year, interfaith program of study called "Emouna l'amphi des religions" (Forum for Faith Religions) at Sciences Po University in Paris. So far, they have trained more than 160 people of all faiths to study various religions. She says, "It shows that religions don't have to fight but can make friends together."[86] Since its founding, this model has inspired other countries, like the Netherlands, Belgium, and Italy to develop similar programs.

Rabbi Bebe is a member of the CCAR, the Central Conference of American Rabbis, the organization that brings together more than 2,000 liberal rabbis around the world. She also helped to found Kerem, the Council of Francophone

Liberal Rabbis. Her aim is to create "a liberal francophone movement with our colleagues in Belgium and Switzerland."[87]

Pauline is a true pioneer. In 2019, she fulfilled one of her goals—to establish the Rabbinical School of Paris, the country's first Reform (liberal) rabbinical school. As of 2022, there were in total only five female rabbis in France. This number is striking when one realizes that France has the third largest Jewish population in the world, after the United States and Israel.[88]

Her message to young people is: "Try to live your dreams and to have a selective ear."[89] She has learned that one must not listen to people who say negative things and try to stop you from pursuing your goals. Through her words and her deeds, Rabbi Pauline Bebe is an example of how a person can make the world a better place.

YAVILAH MCCOY

1972–

BOSTON, USA, 2008

Yavilah was driving slowly along the road and looking for the Costco store. When she stopped for gas, a police car pulled up behind her and started flashing its lights. She got out of her car and headed towards the gas pump, but the white police officer shouted, "Get back in your vehicle!" Yavilah asked, "What's wrong?" He refused to answer but pulled out his gun and yelled, "Get back in your vehicle NOW!" In spite of her fears, Yavilah knew she would have to do something to get out of this terrifying situation.[90]

Yavilah McCoy was born on November 8, 1972, in Brooklyn, New York. She is a fourth-generation Orthodox Jew and member of a third-generation civil rights activist family. She also happens to be a Jew of Color (JOC). (Her family was part of the movement of some African Americans at the turn of the nineteenth century who found religious expression in Judaism.) Both Yavilah's grandparents were engaged in civil rights work to integrate schools, that is, to allow African American children to attend all-white schools. Her grandfather even did security for Dr. Martin Luther King Jr.

Yavilah, whose name comes from "Jubilee" in Hebrew,[91] was raised in the Crown Heights neighborhood in central Brooklyn. By the time Yavilah and her family were living there, most whites had moved to the suburbs. However, the ultra-Orthodox Hasidic Lubavitch Jews had decided to stay. By the 1960s and 1970s, there was a lot of tension between the approximately seventy per cent Black population and the white Lubavitchers in Crown Heights. Yavilah remembers the three-day riot in 1991, and the little boy who lived just down the street who was killed in a traffic accident. Most of the tensions have since died down and people living in Crown Heights today are white, African American, Hispanic, or Latino.

Yavilah and her five siblings grew up in an Orthodox Jewish home. As Yavilah recalls, "My mother was a prolific cook…her challah and her soup… she brought every ounce of southern culinary deliciousness into a kosher kitchen."[92] Both her parents were very invested in Judaism. They encouraged Yavilah to feel strong and proud of who she was. For example, her father studied the *parsha* (weekly Torah reading) with her; her mother welcomed people into their home with open arms. "That was the sun that I grew up in."[93]

Yavilah recalls that when she went to *shul* (synagogue), the majority of the men who prayed there were men of color, with families of color; her home on Shabbat and the holidays was filled with other Jews of color. At home and at synagogue, Yavilah felt loved and a deep sense that Black was beautiful.

However, when Yavilah and her sister went to elementary school and yeshiva high school, she felt disconnected and isolated from the other students, the majority of whom were white. She says, "[There was] a total lack of expectation of my existence; everything was a question and a curiosity."[94] So, from an early age, Yavilah felt "othered" and that she had to constantly explain who she was and where she came from. For example, she remembers how a classmate wouldn't let Yavilah look through her toy microscope because Yavilah was Black.[95] Another time, one of her teachers was amazed that Yavilah, at the age of seven, could read Hebrew and knew the weekly Torah *parsha* (reading). "She's really Jewish!" the teacher said to the principal.

Two teachers, however, helped Yavilah feel accepted: One was Olivia Langston, her primary school teacher. "It was loving on us and giving us a chance to shine…. It created a foundational space where the acceptance I had at home could also be experienced in the Jewish institutional space."[96] The other teacher was Rabbi Leibel Newman, her eighth grade Hebrew teacher and principal of the school. "We felt such a deep respect for him as an educator," Yavilah explains. "He would come close to your desk, he would lean down, he would look you in the eye, and he would go 'excellent.' It made me feel, 'I'm here. This is my place.'"[97]

Yavilah attended the Yeshiva University High School, a girls' Orthodox high school in New York City. Even then, she felt there was more for her in life than what the school slogan proclaimed: "Jewish children today, Jewish mothers tomorrow."[98] After graduating, she continued her studies at Hebrew University in Jerusalem, where she obtained a degree in English education and Judaic studies. She then taught Judaic studies, Hebrew, and English literature in elementary and secondary schools. However, in 2000, Yavilah decided to leave formal teaching and take a new step in her career.

In that year, Yavilah founded an organization called *Ayecha*, which in Hebrew means "Where are you?" (This is, in fact, the question that G-d asks

Adam and Eve when they were hiding after they ate the forbidden fruit.) Yavilah established this organization in order to work with rabbis, synagogues, schools, and Jewish federations to "increase awareness of Jewish diversity and expand inclusion for Jews of color."[99]

In 2006, Yavilah wrote: "We teach people how to understand their Judaism through the lens of race, age, and economic status. When most people think of Jewish, they think white and they think European. But Jews of color have been alive and well for thousands of years in parts of the world."[100] In other words, she wanted to provide training and educational resources to build greater understanding and sensitivity toward Jews of color in the Jewish community.

With offices in St. Louis and New York City, Ayecha provided training and support for Jewish and multiracial families. The organization worked towards helping diverse Jews feel welcomed—in synagogues, schools, neighborhoods, and community centers. Ayecha's programming reached people living in the United States, Canada, England, and Israel. However, in 2009, Yavilah wanted to step back from being *the one* representative of Jews of color. She said at the time: "The idea of associating diversity with a person as opposed to it being a movement within the Jewish community was starting to bother me."[101]

In that same year, Yavilah co-wrote, produced, and performed her one-woman show, *The Colors of Water*. It was a Jewish gospel musical theater work that described the journey of the four generations of women in her Jewish African American family. She described it like this: "*The Colors of Water* provides an exciting evening of edutainment, with moments that make the audience laugh, cry, and sit at the edge of their seats wondering where the journey will take us next."[102]

In 2008, Yavilah became director of the New England Curriculum Initiative (NECI), a non-profit educational consultant organization that provided religious diversity resources to 600 schools in the United States. What does that mean? NECI worked to expand awareness of Jewish identity and culture beyond the idea that Jews are "white and Ashkenazi." The organization helped students understand their Jewish identity in terms of leadership, citizenship, and pursuit of excellence in education. Yavilah believes that "social justice work must transcend the level of words and become fully conscious 'in our *kishkes*'—deep within our bodies."[103]

Yavilah continues to grow and establish new organizations. In 2014, she founded Dimensions Educational Consulting. Yavilah wanted "an organization that would practice racial equity and uphold social justice values within a system, structure, leadership, and culture that centered and empowered Black women's BEING."[104] For example, Dimensions helps leaders develop diversity, equity, and inclusion in their organizations, and support each other while they work for similar goals.

Yavilah has received many awards and honors in her life so far. They include the 2016 Rabbi Marshall T. Meyer Risk Taker Award from the Jews for Racial and Economic Justice organization (JFREJ), and the Spielberg Foundation's Joshua Venture Fellowship. This $100,000 fellowship "supports leaders who create stable organizations that can help grow and transform Jewish life."[105] She was also voted one of "16 Faith Leaders to Watch" by the Center for American Progress in Washington, DC.

Yavilah and her husband, Pinchas, live in Boston and have four children. She continues to speak about the causes that are close to her heart. It is her hope that "...our continued commitment and combined action bring Black liberation, human liberation, and lasting equity and justice closer to a reality for all of us."[106]

JESSICA POSNER ODEDE

1986–

NAIROBI, KENYA, 2007

Jessica had just arrived in Kibera, the biggest slum in Africa. When she saw the rats and the outside toilets, the shacks built of cardboard and corrugated steel, when she smelled the garbage lying in heaps on the muddy paths, she was shocked. "No white person has ever stayed in Kibera," people kept telling her. But she had decided to live there. How else would she be able to help people? Jessica was too stubborn to back down.

When Jessica Posner was born in July 1986 in Denver, Colorado, no one would have imagined what her life's work would turn out to be. She grew up with the basic comforts of a middle-class Jewish family. Her father, David, works as an energy consultant and her mother, Helen, is a clinical psychologist. However, unlike most families in America, Jessica and her younger siblings, Max and Raphaela, grew up without TV or video games. They learned to channel their energy and creativity in different ways.

Jessica didn't have a formal Jewish education, although she did have a bat mitzvah. However, her Jewish upbringing and values affected the choices that she's made in her life. She says, "I believe in justice and fairness, and that we have a collective responsibility to those around us. I hope that I encourage those around me to view the larger picture, empathetically, intellectually and ethically."[107]

When Jessica was about seven years old, she fell in love with the theater. She dreamed of becoming a professional actor. She attended the Denver School of the Arts, a public school from grades six to twelve that attracts young people interested in the arts—music, visual arts, dance, theater, and literature. While she was there, Jessica honed her skills in writing and theater. She applied to a number of prestigious colleges in the United States, and chose Wesleyan University in Middletown, Connecticut, as the place where she wanted to study.

At Wesleyan, Jessica majored in theater and African American studies. She later wrote, "Wesleyan woke me up to the possibility of all there was to learn."[108] In 2007, during her third year at college, Jessica heard about an opportunity to study abroad through the School for International Training, a global non-profit organization that connects thousands of young people with social projects. She was only twenty years old—creative, brave, and determined to make a difference in the world.

One particular project caught her imagination: Shining Hope for Communities (SHOFCO), an organization founded by a young activist called Kennedy Odede, in a part of Nairobi, Kenya, called Kibera.

Kibera is the largest slum or shanty town in Africa and the second largest in the world. More than one and a half million people live there in the direst conditions: no running water or (legal) electricity, few toilets (and the only ones are outside), lack of education, and violent crime. Shacks made of cardboard, salvaged materials, and pieces of corrugated steel line the unpaved, muddy roads; the stink of sewage and garbage fills the air.

Kennedy Odede was born in 1984 and grew up in Kibera with his mother, Jane Achieng, and his seven younger siblings. When he was a child, he suffered abuse from his stepfather as well as dire poverty. Very often, he went to bed hungry. "We could not be full, so we would drink lots of water,"[109] he later wrote. He had only one pair of shorts, and no shirt or shoes. School was an impossible dream, but he learned to read with the help of an older friend and by reading scraps of newspapers he found on the ground.

One day in 2004, as Kennedy was walking along a muddy street in Kibera, a boy offered to sell him a soccer ball. At that time, Kennedy was working ten hours per day as a laborer on a construction site. He earned only one dollar for an entire day's work. He had only twenty cents in his pocket, but he bought the ball. He then gathered together some young people from Kibera to play soccer instead of roaming the streets—perhaps stealing food or money, or drinking and doing drugs. He became convinced that the root of many of the problems in Kibera was the lack of hope.

Kennedy was only twenty-three years old when he founded SHOFCO. From that soccer ball, he developed the idea to try other community projects. One of them was a theater group so that the young people could express their feelings and tell about their lives in a safe place. That's when Jessica's résumé arrived—one that would change both their lives and those of thousands of people in Kibera.

During that summer of 2007, Jessica had emailed her résumé to Kennedy. She hoped he would accept her as a volunteer in SHOFCO. Finally, after many anxious days, she got a reply offering her one semester (four months) as a volunteer for SHOFCO.

When Jessica told her parents that she wanted to go to Kenya, they couldn't understand why. Was this their daughter who hated camping and who packed too much for a weekend trip? Jessica's grandparents, in fact, warned her parents not to let her go to Kenya. But nothing was going to stop Jessica. As her mother, Helen, recalled, "Jessica came into the world the way she is, with a lot of creativity and determination, and she never really looked at obstacles as being obstacles, if it was something she cared about."[110]

When Jessica first arrived in Nairobi, she stayed in a "safe" place on the outskirts of Kibera. She was supposed to live there and commute to her volunteer job in the slum. But she soon realized that she wouldn't be able to work with the young people there unless she lived where they lived. So, she persuaded Kennedy to allow her to move into his tiny shack.

At first, people would crowd around the front door in the morning and ask, "Is the *mzungu* (white person) still alive? Did she survive the night?" She did indeed! And many nights to come. At the same time, Jessica realized that she was different from everyone there, and not just because of the color of her skin. Even if she lived in Kibera, she had the privilege no one else did. She could always leave.

Jessica recognizes how stubborn she is. As she says, "Ever since I was a child, my reaction to the forbidden has been a stubborn desire to keep pushing.... The words *you can't* unleash a determination so intense that at times it even startles me."[111] So, Jessica stayed in Kibera during those difficult months. Even when she got very ill with malaria, she didn't move or run away.

Jessica wanted to use theater as a tool for activism; to make a difference in people's lives. She gathered a group of young people together and encouraged them to tell their stories. She listened as they recounted their lives of violence, rape, poverty, AIDS, and hopelessness. Many of these teenage girls already had one or two children; they had little hope of supporting them.

Using their stories, Jessica helped Kennedy and his friends write scripts for their street theater plays, which the group performed all over Kenya—in community centers, libraries, sidewalks, the national theater, even at a political rally attended by both presidential candidates before the election that year. Everywhere they went, they were greeted with positive words and applause.

Although Jessica returned to Wesleyan after the semester was over, she was different from most volunteers who work overseas. She knew she had changed; that her perspective about the world had changed. She returned to Kenya the following year to continue her work in Kibera. She graduated Phi Beta Kappa (an honorary society in the US that recognizes high academic achievement) in African American studies from Wesleyan in 2009.

Jessica and Kennedy had developed a strong relationship—personal and professional—during Jessica's first stay in Kibera. In 2007, when Jessica learned that Kennedy's life was in danger during the violence of postelection Kenya,[112] she helped him escape. She even helped him get a full scholarship to Wesleyan. He graduated with full honors in sociology and government in 2012. He was the first person from Kibera to receive a university degree.

Through living and working together, Kennedy and Jessica fell deeply in love. After Kennedy's graduation, they traveled to Denver where they were married. They then returned to Nairobi to continue and expand SHOFCO's work.

SHOFCO has helped thousands of people in Kibera and also in another slum near Nairobi called Mathare. Its first project was to establish the Kibera

School for Girls. (The school is free but the parents have to commit to working five weeks during the year instead of paying tuition.) Jessica and Kennedy firmly believe that girls are tomorrow's leaders; given the right tools, they can lead themselves and their families out of poverty.

It was a huge financial struggle to establish the girls' school. With Jessica's help, they found some generous donors for the project, but she often wasn't sure it would actually get off the ground. One of the school songs includes the words:

> *I'm here to tell you: I too have my rights,*
> *A right to live, a right to eat,*
> *A right to dress, and a right to education.*[113]

Other projects for the whole community came as a result of that first one, and were created mostly by community members working together: clean water, electricity, toilets, free health care for mothers and children, and a community center. SHOFCO also offers what it calls "community empowerment" projects. It helps people, especially women, by offering them small loans to start a small business, free computer and library services, and adult education classes. Jessica would probably be gratified to hear that George Okewa, a Kibera community leader, has said, "She has eaten as the locals, she has lived as the locals. They see her as one of them."[114]

For her work, Jessica has received many honors and awards. In 2010, she won the Do Something Award and was named "America's top world changer under 25." She has also received the Echoing Green Fellowship, the Dell Social Innovation Competition, the Clinton Global Initiative, and the David Rockefeller Bridging Leadership Award. All these awards help to fund various SHOFCO projects.

Jessica has continued to spread the word about SHOFCO. She's been interviewed for magazines like *Vogue* and *Good Housekeeping*, and newspapers like

The New York Times. She and Kennedy have given a number of inspiring (and funny) TED Talks. In addition to all their activities, the couple's four children keep them busy.

In 2019, Jessica took on a new and demanding role. She became the CEO (chief executive officer) of the international non-profit organization called Girl Effect. This organization reaches millions of girls in over twenty countries in Africa and Asia. Its website says, "It's time girls had the freedom to be their confident and curious selves. It's time to arm girls with the skills to negotiate and redefine what they are told is possible."[115]

Jessica Posner Odede has accomplished much in her life so far. How much more will she be able to do to help girls and women all over the world?

GLOSSARY

Anschluss: The forcible uniting of Germany and Austria in 1938.

Antisemitism: Hostility toward or discrimination against Jews as a religious, ethnic, or racial group.

Apartheid: The former policy of segregation and political, social, and economic discrimination against the non-white majority in the Republic of South Africa.

Ashkenazim: Jews who lived in the Rhineland valley and in neighboring France before their migration eastward to Slavic lands (e.g., Poland, Lithuania, Russia) after the Crusades (11th–13th century) and their descendants.

Bat mitzvah: A Jewish girl who at twelve or more years of age assumes religious responsibilities.

Brit milah: The ceremony during which a circumcision is performed on Jewish baby boys when they are eight days old. Girls have a separate baby naming ceremony.

Camelot: The site of King Arthur's palace and court; a time, place, or atmosphere of idyllic happiness.[116]

Chutzpah: Supreme self-confidence; nerve, gall.

Communism: The system in which goods are owned in common and are available to all as needed.

The Final Solution: The Nazi program for extermination of all Jews in Europe.

The Holocaust: The mass slaughter of European civilians and especially Jews by the Nazis during World War II.

Kristallnacht: The Night of Broken Glass was the violent, planned destruction of Jewish businesses and synagogues carried out by the Nazi Party's Sturmabteilung paramilitary forces with the participation of civilians and Hitler Youth throughout Nazi Germany on November 9 and 10, 1938.

NAACP: National Association for the Advancement of Colored People.

Operation Moses: The covert evacuation of Ethiopian Jews to Israel from Sudan during a civil war that caused a famine in 1984.

Pale of Settlement: A territory within the borders of czarist Russia (1721 to 1917) where Jews were allowed to live and beyond which they were mostly forbidden.

Parsha: The section of the Torah assigned for weekly reading in synagogue worship.

Pogrom: The organized massacre of helpless people, specifically Jews.

Quota system: During the 1930s, some countries like Hungary, Poland, and even Canada allowed only a small number of Jews to study professions like medicine and law.

Seder: A dinner usually held in a Jewish home on the first and second nights of Passover when Jews tell the story of their freedom from slavery in Egypt.

Sephardim: European Jews who settled in Spain and Portugal and later in the Balkans, North Africa, England, the Netherlands, and the Americas.

TED Talk: A short presentation that focuses on technology, entertainment, and/or design.

SOURCES CONSULTED

(*SUITABLE FOR YOUNG PEOPLE)

ÁGNES KELETI

BOOKS

Sándor, Dávid, and Dobor Dezső. *100 Years of Ágnes Keleti, The Queen of Gymnastics*. Budapest: Hungarian Gymnastics Federation, 2020.

WEBSITES

Ingle, Jean. "Ágnes Keleti: Olympic great who fled Nazis and Soviets smashes 100 barrier." *Guardian*, Jan. 11, 2021.

O'Kane, Caitlin. "'I love life': Agnes Keleti, Holocaust survivor and oldest Olympic champion, reflects on 100th birthday." *CBS News*, Jan. 12, 2021.

Sobovitz, Jacov. "Agnes Keleti." *Shalvi/Hyman Encyclopedia of Jewish Women*. December 31, 1999. Jewish Women's Archive.

RUTH FIRST

BOOKS

*Denenberg, Barry. *Nelson Mandela: No Easy Walk to Freedom.* New York: Scholastic, 2014 (First published 1991).

*Downing, David. *Apartheid in South Africa.* Witness to History. Chicago: Heinemann, 2004.

First, Ruth. *117 Days: An Account of Confinement and Interrogation under the South African 90-Day Detention Law.* New York: Penguin Random House, 2009. (First published 1956.)

First, Ruth. *Ruth First: Voices of Liberation.* Ed. Don Pinnock. Cape Town, South Africa: HSRC Press, 2012.

Mandela, Nelson. *Long Walk to Freedom: The Autobiography of Nelson Mandela.* New York: Little, Brown & Company, 2013. First published 1994.

Slovo, Gillian. *Every Secret Thing: My Family, My Country.* Boston: Little, Brown & Company, 1997.

Wieder, Alan. *Ruth First and Joe Slovo in the War to End Apartheid.* New York: Monthly Review Press, 2013.

WEBSITES

"In the Psychiatrist's Chair – Gillian Slovo, Interview by Dr. Anthony Clare." BBC. BBC Sounds, 1997.

"RF/6: Don Pinnock Interview with Robyn Slovo." Ruth First Papers, 1990.

"Rockel Interviews." Ruth First Papers, 2012.

Shain, Milton, and Miriam Pimstone. "Ruth First." Jewish Women's Archive, December 31, 1999.

DVDS AND VIDEOS

A World Apart. Directed by Chris Menges. Written by Shawn Slovo. Atlantic Entertainment and British Screen, 1988.

Catch a Fire. Directed by Phillip Noyce. Written by Shawn Slovo. Working Title Films, 2006.

*Invictus. Directed by Clint Eastwood. Warner Video, 2009.

MARION WIESEL

BOOKS

*Epstein, Nadine (ed.). *Elie Wiesel: An Extraordinary Life and Legacy*. Washington, DC: Moment Books, 2019.

Wiesel, Elie. *All Rivers Run to the Sea: Memoirs*. New York: Alfred A. Knopf, 1995.

WEBSITES

"Marion Wiesel Tribute: Child of Europe." YouTube, February 4, 2021.

"Marion Wiesel—Social Justice Warrior." YouTube, February 10, 2021.

Elie Wiesel Foundation for Humanity.

Henerson, Evan T. "Charity Benefit Honors Marion Wiesel on Her 90th Birthday." Zenger News, February 5, 2021.

Levine, Daniel S. "Marion Wiesel, Elie's Wife: 5 Fast Facts You Need to Know." *Heavy*, July 3, 2016.

ARTICLES

Ann Landis. "They Knocked on our Door." Personal memoir of Ann Landis, ca. 1960s. Used with permission.

INTERVIEWS

Elisha Wiesel, interview with the author, November 23, 2021 and November 29, 2021.

Marion Wiesel, interview with the author, December 20, 2021.

RITA ARDITTI

BOOKS

Arditti, Rita. *Searching for Life: The Grandmothers of Plaza de Mayo and the Disappeared Children of Argentina.* Oakland, CA: University of California Press, 1999.

Arditti, Rita, Renate Klein, and Shelley Minden. *Test-Tube Women: What Future for Motherhood.* New York: Routledge, 1989. First published 1984.

WEBSITES

Disch, Estelle. "Raquel Rita Arditti, 1934–2009: A Life of Activism: Science, Feminism, Health, and Human Rights." Rita Arditti.

Disch, Estelle. "Rita Arditti." *Shalvi/Hyman Encyclopedia of Jewish Women,* June 23, 2021. Jewish Women's Archive.

Muchnik, Federico. "Rita Arditti: Activist, Biologist, Teacher: 1934–2009." Jewish Women's Archive.

DVDS AND VIDEOS

Abuelas: Grandmothers on a Mission. Directed by Naomi Weis. New York: Women Make Movies, 2012. Spanish with English subtitles. 28 min.

Arditti Tribute: Lisa Baldez Speaks. Vimeo.

Catherine Russo interviewed Rita for her film, *A Moment in Her Story*, about the Second Wave of the feminist movement in Boston in the 1960s and 1970s.

Estelle Disch speaks about the life and work of Rita Arditti. Vimeo.

Federico Muchnik speaks about his mother, Rita Arditti. Vimeo.

Video Tribute. Directed by Federico Muchnik, 2010. 12 min.

INTERVIEWS

Estelle Disch, interview with the author, October 26, 2021.

Federico Muchnik, interview with the author, October 29, 2021.

MARIKA GIDALI

BOOKS

Otero, Decio. *Marika Gidali: Singular e Plural.* São Paulo: Editora Senac, 2001.

WEBSITES

Ballet Stagium: Wikipedia.

Falbel, Anat and Nachman Falbel. "Marika Gidali." *Shalvi/Hyman Encyclopedia of Jewish Women*, June 23, 2021. Jewish Women's Archive.

"Marika Gidali." *Persona em Foco.* Transl. Fabio Sena, with the assistance of Lynn Westerhout. Interviewed by Cassia Navas and Regina Helena de Paiva Ramos, July 26, 2017.

Project Vozes do Holocausto: Um legado para o futuro [Voices of the Holocaust: A legacy for the future]. Transl. Andre Sena. Interviewed by Rachel Mizrahi. São Paulo: University of São Paulo, July 20, 2017.

JUDY FELD CARR

BOOKS

*Arato, Rona. *Courage and Compassion: Ten Canadians Who Made a Difference.* Toronto: Owlkids, 2008.

Troper, Harold. *The Ransomed of God: The Remarkable Story of One Woman's Role in the Rescue of Syrian Jews.* Toronto: Malcolm Lester Books, 1999.

WEBSITES

Troper, Harold and Susan Landau-Clark. "Judy Feld Carr." *Shalvi/Hyman Encyclopedia of Jewish Women.* 23 June 2021. Jewish Women's Archive.

DVDS AND VIDEOS

"Judy Feld Carr – Miss Judy," directed by Eyal Tavor, Dec. 17, 2013. YouTube.

INTERVIEWS

Judy Feld Carr, interview with the author, December 14, 2021.

ROSALIE SILBERMAN ABELLA

BOOKS

*Favilli, Elena. *Goodnight Stories for Rebel Girls: 100 Immigrant Women Who Changed the World.* Italy: Timbuktu Labs, 2020.

*Sharp, Rosalie, Irving Abella, and Edwin Goodwin, eds. *Growing Up Jewish: Canadians Tell Their Own Stories.* Toronto: McClelland & Stewart, 1997.

WEBSITES

Abella, Irving. "Rosalie Silberman Abella." *Shalvi/Hyman Encyclopedia of Jewish Women*, December 31, 1999. Jewish Women's Archive.

Ankita Gupta, "Judicial Biography: Justice Rosalie Abella," August 29, 2019, The Court.

Nurse, Donna Bailey. "Just 'Rosie.'" *University of Toronto Magazine*, December 20, 2005.

Paul Wells. "Rosie Abella Said She'd Answer Questions When She Turned 75." *Maclean's*, June 15, 2021.

DVDS AND VIDEOS

Abella, Rosalie. "Inaugural Elie Wiesel Lectureship in Human Rights." The Raoul Wallenberg Centre for Human Rights, Dec. 9, 2020. Facebook.

"The Hon. Rosalie Silberman Abella Bids Farewell to the Supreme Court." Supreme Court of Canada, 2021.

"Madame Justice Steps Down." YouTube. *The Agenda*, 2021.

PAULINE BEBE

WEBSITES

"Pauline Bebe." Jewish Women's Archive.

"Notre Rabbin Pauline Bebe." CJL, Paris Ile-de-France.

"Religion. Les Espoirs De Pauline Bebe, Première Femme Rabbin Française." *Le Progrès*, April 1, 2011.

Steinkopf-Frank, Hannah. "Women Rabbis in France Carve Their Own Path." *Religion Unplugged*, November 3, 2021.

DVDS AND VIDEOS

"L'invitée Du 12/13 Pauline Bebe Sur RCJ." YouTube. Radio RCJ, 2019.

"Le Gros Journal De Pauline Bebe: La Première Femme Rabbin De France." YouTube. Clique TV, 2017.

"Le Rabbin Pauline Bebe est la Première Femme à avoir été Ordonnée Rabbin." Dailymotion, 2011.

"Pauline Bebe–Le XXIe Siècle Sera Théologique!" YouTube, 2019.

"Pauline Bebe: Most Beautiful Moment." YouTube. Jewish Women's Archive, 2016.

"Pauline Bebe: My Judaism is Your Judaism." YouTube. Jewish Women's Archive, 2016.

"Pauline Bebe: The Fight to Be a Rabbi." YouTube. Jewish Women's Archive, 2016.

INTERVIEW

Rabbi Pauline Bebe, interview with the author, Feb. 8, 2022.

YAVILAH MCCOY

BOOKS

Haynes, Bruce D. *The Soul of Judaism: Jews of African Descent in America*. New York: New York University Press, 2018.

WEBSITES

"Yavilah McCoy." Jewish Women's Archive.

Dimensions Educational Consulting.

Gillick, Jeremy January. "A Voice for Jews of Color." *The Forward*, January 29, 2009.

Gray, Helen T. "Yavilah McCoy Has a Story to Tell That Spans Generation." *The Kansas City Star*, September 29, 2006.

McCoy, Yavilah. "Why the Purim Story Gives Me Hope That Our Nation Can Make Black Lives Matter." *HuffPost*, May 13, 2015.

DVDS AND VIDEOS

"JWFNY Convening 2020 Day 1: Jewish Intersectionality." YouTube. Jewish Women's Foundation of New York, 2020.

"Yavilah McCoy: The Deal with Nissim Black." YouTube, 2021.

JESSICA POSNER ODEDE

BOOKS

Nicholas D. Kristof and Sheryl WuDunn. *A Path Appears: Transforming Lives, Creating Opportunity*. New York: Knopf, 2014.

Odede, Kennedy and Jessica Posner. *Find Me Unafraid: Love, Loss, and Hope in an African Slum*. New York: HarperCollins Publishers, 2015.

WEBSITES

Girl Effect.

"Jessica Posner Odede." Jewish Women's Archive.

"Jessica Posner Odede." SHOFCO.

Moore, John. "Jessica Posner: Changing Lives in a Hell on Earth." *The Denver Post*, July 4, 2010 (updated May 6, 2016).

Moore, John. "Posner's Triumphant Tale Is a World-Changer and a Page-Turner." *The Denver Post*, July 4, 2010 (updated May 6, 2016).

"Women at Work: Jess Posner Odede." *Vanity Fair*, July 15, 2021.

DVDS AND VIDEOS

A Path Appears. Independent Lens, PBS, 2015.

"Jessica Posner and Kennedy Odede Join Larry King on PoliticKING | Larry King Now | Ora.TV." YouTube. Larry King, 2015.

"Jessica Posner Odede." YouTube, 2021.

"The Shining Hope of Kibera–Kennedy Odede." YouTube. Engage Talk, 2018.

"What Forgiveness Can Offer | Kennedy Odede and Jessica Posner Odede." YouTube. TED Archive, 2017.

ACKNOWLEDGMENTS

This book could not have been written without the help, support, and cooperation of many people. Firstly, I'd like to thank the women and their families whom I interviewed. They contributed their time and energy to add a personal dimension to my writing: Federico Muchnik (Rita Arditti's son), Estelle Disch (Rita Arditti's partner), Rabbi Pauline Bebe, Judy Feld Carr, Yavilah McCoy, Jessica Posner Odede, Elisha Wiesel (Marion Wiesel's son), Marion Wiesel, and Mark L. Landis (Marion Wiesel's nephew).

Other people helped along the way—many with a comment that sparked further exploration: Cecile Freeman, Barbara Glaser, Janet Horowitz, Rose Kamnitzer, Myrna Levy, and Arthur Zuckerman. I'd like to give a special thanks to Fabio and Andre Sena, who skilfully translated Marika Gidali's online interviews from Portuguese.

My writers' group always keeps me on track with their honest and insightful feedback: Rona Arato, Sydell Waxman, Lynn Westerhout, and Frieda Wishinsky.

The wonderful women at Second Story Press, who help to make every book the best it can be: Gillian Rodgerson (managing editor), Laura Atherton (production manager), Natasha Bozorgi (copy editor), Emma Rodgers (sales and marketing), Phuong Truong (general manager), and of course, Margie Wolfe (publisher), who always adds her strength and passion to whatever I dream of writing.

Last but not least, I'd like to thank my editor, Erin Della Mattia, for her perceptive editing of this book. She asked some tough questions and made me think more deeply about these women's lives, as well as occasionally adding a positive "Wow!" to her comments.

Thank you all for helping to tell the stories of these ten amazing women.

ABOUT THE AUTHOR

Anne Dublin is a former teacher-librarian and award-winning author living in Toronto. She has a particular interest in Jewish history and has written biographies of June Callwood and Bobbie Rosenfeld, as well as the collective biography *Dynamic Women Dancers*. She is also the author of the children's historical fiction novels *The Orphan Rescue, 44 Hours or Strike!, A Cage Without Bars,* and *Jacob and the Mandolin Adventure*.

ENDNOTES

1   Nicholas D. Kristof, *A Path Appears: Transforming Lives, Creating Opportunity* (New York: Alfred A. Knopf, 2014), frontispiece.

2   Kravitz, Leonard and Kerry M. Olitzky (ed. and transl.), *Pirke Avot: A Modern Commentary on Jewish Ethics* (New York: UAHC Press, 1993), 30.

3   Dávid Sándor and Dobor Dezső, *100 Years of Ágnes Keleti, The Queen of Gymnastics* (Budapest: Hungarian Gymnastics Federation, 2020), 106.

4   Sándor and Dezső, *100 Years of Ágnes Keleti*, 136–7.

5   Sándor and Dezső, *100 Years of Ágnes Keleti*, 629.

6   Ágnes Keleti, interview by Caitlin O'Kane, *CBS News*, January 12, 2021.

7   Nelson Mandela, *Long Walk to Freedom: The Autobiography of Nelson Mandela* (New York: Little, Brown & Company, 2013), 91.

8   Gillian Slovo, *Every Secret Thing: My Family, My Country* (Boston: Little, Brown & Company, 1997), 35.

9   Slovo, *Every Secret Thing*, 35.

10   Slovo, *Every Secret Thing*, 40.

11   Slovo, *Every Secret Thing*, 43.

12   Gillian Slovo, interview by Dr. Anthony Clare, "In the Psychiatrist's Chair," *BBC Sounds*, Aug. 10, 1997.

13   Ruth First, "The Cell," in *Ruth First: Voices of Liberation*, ed. Don Pinnock (Cape Town, South Africa: HSRC Press, 2012), 152–3.

14   Ruth First, *Ruth First: Voices of Liberation*, ed. Don Pinnock (Cape Town, South Africa: HSRC Press, 2012), 21.

15   Slovo, *Every Secret Thing*, 116.

16   Slovo, *Every Secret Thing*, 120.

17   Pinnock, *Ruth First*, 3.

18   Marion Wiesel, interview with the author, Dec. 20, 2021.

19   "Marion Wiesel Tribute," YouTube, Feb. 4, 2021.

20   Ibid.

21   Ibid.

22   Marion Wiesel, interview with the author, Dec. 20, 2021.

23   Ann Landis, *They Knocked on Our Door*, 1960s, personal memoir.

24   Mark Landis in "Marion Erster: Child of Europe," YouTube, Feb. 4, 2021.

25   Landis, *They Knocked on Our Door.*

26   Landis, *They Knocked on Our Door.*

27   Marion Wiesel, interview with the author, Dec. 20, 2021.

28   "Marion Wiesel Tribute," YouTube, Feb. 4, 2021.

29   "Charity Benefit Honors Marion Wiesel on Her 90th Birthday," *The Tennessee Tribune*, Feb. 5, 2021.

30   Elie Wiesel, *All Rivers Run to the Sea: Memoirs* (New York, Alfred A. Knopf, 1995), 338.

31   "Marion Wiesel: Social Justice Warrior," YouTube, Feb. 10, 2021.

32   Ibid.

33   The Nobel Peace Prize, 1986.

34   "Charity Benefit Honors Marion Wiesel on Her 90th Birthday," *The Tennessee Tribune*, Feb. 5, 2021.

35   Rita Arditti, *Searching for Life: The Grandmothers of Plaza de Mayo and the Disappeared Children of Argentina* (Oakland: University of California Press, 1999), 3.

36   Federico Muchnik, interview with the author, Oct. 29, 2021.

37   Arditti, Klein and Minden, *Test-Tube Women: What Future for Motherhood* (New York: Routledge, 1989), 2.

38   Federico Muchnik, interview with the author, Oct. 29, 2021.

39   Estelle Disch, interview with the author, Oct. 26, 2021.

40   *The Tribe of Dina: A Jewish Women's Anthology*, ed. Melanie Kaye Kantrowitz and Irena Klepfisz (Boston: Beacon Press, 1989).

41   Federico Muchnik, interview with the author, Oct. 29, 2021.

42   "Arditti Tribute: Lisa Baldez Speaks," April 17, 2012.

43   Anat Falbel and Nachman Falbel, "Marika Gidali," *Shalvi/Hyman Encyclopedia of Jewish Women*, June 23, 2021. Jewish Women's Archive.

44   Marika Gidali, *Entrevista Marika Gidali [Voices of the Holocaust: a legacy for the future]*, São Paulo: University of São Paulo, July 20, 2017.

45   Marika Gidali, email to the author, June 22, 2022.

46   Marika Gidali, *Persona em Foco [Person in Focus]*, July 26, 2017.

47   Marika Gidali, *Entrevista Marika Gidali*, July 20, 2017.

48   Ibid.

49   Marika Gidali, *Persona em Foco [Person in Focus]*, July 26, 2017.

50   Marika Gidali, *Entrevista Marika Gidali*, July 20, 2017.

51   Decio Otero, *Marika Gidali: Singular e Plural*, (São Paulo: Editora Senac, 2001), 181.

52   Marika Gidali, *Entrevista Marika Gidali*, July 20, 2017.

53   Marika Gidali, *Persona em Foco [Person in Focus]*, July 26, 2017.

54   Ibid.

55   Marika Gidali, *Entrevista Marika Gidali*, July 20, 2017.

56   Judy Feld Carr, interview with the author, December 14, 2021.

57   Ibid.

58   Ibid.

59   "Judy Feld Carr – Miss Judy," YouTube, Dec. 17, 2013.

60   Judy Feld Carr, interview with the author, December 14, 2021.

61   Rona Arato, *Courage and Compassion: Ten Canadians Who Made a Difference* (Toronto: Owlkids, 2008), 63.

62   "Judy Feld Carr – Miss Judy," YouTube, Dec. 17, 2013.

63   Harold Troper, *The Ransomed of God: The Remarkable Story of One Woman's Role in the Rescue of Syrian Jews* (Toronto: Malcolm Lester Books, 1999), 70.

64   "Judy Feld Carr – Miss Judy," YouTube, Dec. 17, 2013.

65   Troper, *The Ransomed of God*, 126.

66   "Judy Feld Carr – Miss Judy," YouTube, Dec. 17, 2013.

67   Troper, *The Ransomed of God*, 143.

68   "Judy Feld Carr – Miss Judy," YouTube, Dec. 17, 2013.

69   Ibid.

70   Troper, *The Ransomed of God*, 238.

71   Troper, *The Ransomed of God*, 5.

72   Elena Favilli, *Goodnight Stories for Rebel Girls: 100 Immigrant Women Who Changed the World* (Italy: Timbuktu Labs, 2020), 161.

73   Rosalie Sharp, Irving Abella, and Edwin Goodwin (eds.), *Growing Up Jewish: Canadians Tell Their Own Stories* (Toronto: McClelland & Stewart, 1997), 217.

74   Paul Wells, "Rosie Abella said she'd answer questions when she turned 75," *Macleans*, June 15, 2021.

75   "Madame Justice Steps Down," interview by Steve Paikin, *The Agenda with Steve Paikin*, TVO, July 1, 2021.

76   Supreme Court of Canada—Webcast—The Hon. Rosalie Silberman Abella bids farewell to the Supreme Court.

77   ARCH Disability Law Centre, History.

78   Rosalie Abella, "Inaugural Elie Wiesel Lectureship in Human Rights," The Raoul Wallenberg Centre for Human Rights, Dec. 9, 2020.

79   Pauline Bebe, interview with the author, Feb. 8, 2022.

80   Ibid.

81   Ibid.

82   "L'invitée du 12/13 Pauline Bebe sur RCJ," YouTube, Dec. 19, 2019.

83　"Religion: The hopes of Pauline Bebe, the first French woman rabbi," interview by Nicolas Ballet, April 1, 2011, Religion. Les espoirs de Pauline Bebe, première femme rabbin française (leprogres.fr).

84　Ibid.

85　Pauline Bebe, interview with the author, Feb. 8, 2022.

86　Ibid.

87　"Religion: The hopes of Pauline Bebe, the first French woman rabbi," interview by Nicolas Ballet, April 1, 2011, Religion. Les espoirs de Pauline Bebe, première femme rabbin française.

88　The first woman rabbi was ordained in the US in 1972.

89　Pauline Bebe, interview with the author, Feb. 8, 2022.

90　"I was innocent and afraid for my life," Jewish Telegraph Agency, June 3, 2020.

91　The jubilee is the 50th year of celebration that comes after seven cycles of harvest, where, traditionally in Jewish law and in the land of Israel, all slaves go free and all debts are repaid.

92　Quoted in "Yavilah McCoy | The Deal with Nissim Black (Full Episode)," YouTube (viewed March 20, 2022).

93　Ibid.

94　Ibid.

95　Yavilah McCoy, keynote address, JOFEE Network Gathering, Sept. 1, 2019, Petaluma, California.

96   Quoted in "Yavilah McCoy | The Deal with Nissim Black (Full Episode)," YouTube (viewed March 20, 2022).

97   Ibid.

98   Yavilah McCoy, keynote address, JOFEE Network Gathering.

99   "Yavilah McCoy," Jewish Women's Archive.

100   "Yavilah McCoy has a story to tell that spans generations," *The Kansas City Star*, September 19, 2006.

101   Jeremy Gillick, "A voice for Jews of color," *Forward*, January 28, 2009.

102   "Yavilah McCoy – Biography," JewAge.

103   Yavilah McCoy, Judaism Unbound Podcast, Episode 155 – The Women's March.

104   "Mission & Vision," Dimensions Educational Consulting.

105   Bruce D. Haynes, *The Soul of Judaism* (New York: New York University Press, 2018), 219.

106   "Why the Purim Story Gives Me Hope that Our Nation Can Make Black Lives Matter," Yavilah McCoy, *HuffPost*, May 13, 2015.

107   Jessica Posner Odede, email to author, March 23, 2022.

108   Kennedy Odede and Jessica Posner. *Find Me Unafraid: Love, Loss, and Hope in an African Slum* (New York: HarperCollins Publishers, 2015), 8.

109   Kennedy Odede, quoted in Nicholas D. Kristof and Sheryl WuDunn, *A Path Appears: Transforming Lives, Creating Opportunity* (New York: Alfred A. Knopf, 2014), 130.

110   John Moore, "Jessica Posner: Changing Lives in a Hell on Earth," *The Denver Post*, July 4, 2010 (updated May 6, 2016).

111   Odede and Posner, *Find Me Unafraid*, 19.

112   Many people thought the election had been rigged and they didn't agree with the announced results.

113   Kristof and WuDunn, *A Path Appears*, 138.

114   George Okewa, quoted in Kristof and WuDunn, *A Path Appears*, 140.

115   Girl Effect website.

116   *Merriam-Webster Dictionary.*